GOD IS GENIUS

Spiritual Devotions for Your Personal Transformation, Breakthroughs, and Miracles

Rahfeal Gordon

Madison + Park Agency

Written by Rahfeal Gordon

Published by Madison + Park

979-8-9956285-0-7 (Hardcover)

979-8-9956285-1-4 (Softcover)

Published 2026

United States of America

This book is dedicated to God.

Thank you for refining me.

Making me into new wine and pouring me into new skin.

TABLE OF CONTENTS

SECTION IV:

TRANSFORMATION & PURPOSE

Living It Out

SECTION V:

WALKING WITH GOD DAILY

Sustained Faith

INTRODUCTION

A Devotional Written in the Wilderness

God broke me down. God stripped me of everything I thought I needed. God left me in the wilderness long enough for me to remember something I had forgotten .... He was the only one I ever truly needed to depend on. I had to feel completely lost before I could be found again. I had to watch the old version of myself die so that God could breathe life into a new one.

For a little over two years, my life felt like wave after wave of loss. Every time I thought I could catch my breath, another hit came. Eventually I reached a point where I had nothing left to fight with — nothing left to lean on except God. And that's when I finally surrendered and told Him, "You lead. I'm done trying to drive my own life."

It started with something that, at first, felt small, but it shook my world.

My hard drive crashed.

That one hard drive carried more than twenty years of my work as a speaker and entrepreneur. My ideas. My presentations. My notes. My vision. My life's work. And just like that... it was gone. No backup. No second copy. No miracle recovery.

Just silence.

I had to sit with the realization that two decades of work had disappeared in a moment. I remember staring at the screen, almost hoping it would magically come back to life. But it didn't.

And before I could even process that loss, life delivered another one.

One Sunday morning, while I was on my way to church, I got a call from New Jersey. My mother was in the bathroom in so much pain she couldn't move. I wasn't even in New Jersey at the time, so all I could do was give instructions over the phone to her boyfriend and tell him to call an ambulance and keep me updated.

A week later, the news came.

Stage 4 cancer.

That diagnosis hit like a punch to the chest. Everything slowed down. Everything became real in a way that words can't fully describe.

That was in September.

And just weeks later, Friday, October 13th, close to three o'clock in the morning, my mother took her last breath. The pain of that moment is something I can't fully explain. The woman who carried me for nine months… the woman who made the decision to bring me into this world so I could experience this life… was gone.

Just like that.

No amount of success, strength, or faith prepares you for that kind of loss. And in that season, standing in the middle of grief, confusion, and brokenness, I realized something that changed me forever:

Sometimes God allows everything around you to fall apart so that you finally realize He is the only foundation that was holding you up the entire time.

But I kept praying.

I kept praising.

I kept asking God for strength and guidance because I was going through something I had never experienced before. I was hurting in places that nobody could see. And just when I thought the wilderness couldn't get any deeper, harder, or more painful, God reminded me of something powerful:

The wilderness will test you.

Test after test.
Trial after trial.

But one thing is certain, when you belong to God, He will keep you. He will cover you. He will protect you even when everything around you feels like it's falling apart.

My mother passed away on Friday.

Four days later, I was on a plane headed to Indonesia to fulfill a speaking engagement.

Even now, I cannot fully explain how I did it. The only way I can describe it is that I was operating in the Spirit. There is no other explanation for how a grieving son could get on a plane and fly 25 hours across the world, stand in front of a large audience, pour into people, and then three days later get back on another flight for another 26-hour journey to New Jersey to continue planning the burial of his mother.

My body was there, but my spirit was carrying me.

After we buried my mother, another loss followed. Two months later, in December, her boyfriend passed away. We believe it was from a broken heart.

Loss after loss.

I was exhausted.

I felt like I had been in constant motion with no time to breathe, no time to rest, no time to truly process the grief that was sitting on my chest like a heavy weight.

When I finally returned home in January, I thought I would find rest and solitude. But that season had other plans for me. The only thing I could find myself doing was reading the Bible daily, writing devotionals, and journaling whenever the emotions became too heavy to hold inside.

Day after day.
Night after night.

I wrote.

At the time, I was living in a beautiful residence, but behind the scenes my life was shifting in ways I never imagined. My global speaking tour had been put on hold because I chose to spend time with my mother during the final season of her life. On top of that, the crash of my hard drive meant losing nearly all of my business files.

Grief has a way of clouding your mind. It makes even the smallest decisions feel heavy.

My business began going through a rough patch. My personal finances followed. So, when I returned home, I began reaching out to my network and researching ways to find temporary financial support while I got back on my feet.

An organization stepped in and offered assistance.

But when they reached out to my property management to provide payment, payment that would have helped me maintain my home and give me a few months of breathing room, management declined the check.

They knew everything I was dealing with.

And yet they turned down every resource that tried to help me.

That season taught me one of the hardest lessons of my life:

Some people will smile in your face, ask for your help when they need you, and gladly use your resources but when your storm comes, they will stand on the sidelines and watch you drown.

There were family members, friends, and people who knew exactly what I was facing who simply didn't keep their word. Some were quick to talk about my situation with others, but slow to show up for me when I needed them most.

But what they didn't realize was this: Even in the middle of the chaos, God was still protecting me.

Yes, I was losing things around me, but God was growing something inside of me. God was creating new space in my life. Eventually I had to face something I never imagined would happen to me - an eviction.

I had to leave the place I had called home for six years.

At that moment, I couldn't understand why everything seemed to be hitting me from every direction. But even in that confusion, I kept praying. I kept asking God to guide my steps and show me where to go.

And I kept writing.

Right after the eviction, I had to go into surgery just a few days later. I was still grieving. Still hurting. Still trying to understand everything that had happened. Friends stepped in to help me heal physically, mentally, and spiritually. During that time, I moved seven different times in a short few months while trying to recover from surgery and navigate the storm of my life.

There were moments when the weight of everything became overwhelming. Moments where I felt embarrassed. Moments when I felt ashamed for needing help because I had always been the one helping others.

When it felt like every resource had been exhausted, I checked into a small hotel that I could barely afford. The representative I spoke with on the phone did something I will never forget. They gave me their employee family-and-friends discount just so I could stay there.

Even in the wilderness, God will send strangers to remind you that He sees you. Those days in that hotel were some of the hardest of my life.

They were painful.
They were humbling.

I remember asking God, "Why would you allow me to be in this place after all the success, money, awards, and high-level connections. I don't deserve this." But even in that season, I kept worshiping.

I played gospel music.
I read my Bible.
I wrote my devotionals.

I began speaking healing, prosperity, and breakthrough over my life. I realized something powerful during that season: I couldn't run through it. I had to walk through it. I had to stand tall even while my heart was hurting and walk THROUGH it. I had to lift my head and remind myself that this season would not define my life.

During that time, I found myself speaking with my father more often. Our relationship had not always been the closest, but over the years we had begun healing and rebuilding. And in that season, he became a source of wisdom for me.

He would often say to me, "Hey Rah Rah… keep God first in everything you do."

Those were simple words, but they carried deep meaning. He would call me randomly and share how much I was on his mind and end his call saying, "I love you."

One day, we were having a father and son conversation about relationships, and he told me something that stayed with me: *"Trust and loyalty are everything. If someone can't be trusted, there can be no loyalty. And if someone isn't loyal, there can be no trust. No matter what anyone tells you."*

Those words stayed with me, especially during a time when I had to make the difficult decision to let go of someone I was dating while I was walking through what I now call my 'Job Season.'

For a while, my father helped me get through some difficult months after my mother passed.

But then he started getting sick.

Not even a year later, he began going in and out of the hospital because of heart complications. His heart was getting weaker.

While he was in the hospital, I was often the only person he would call. He didn't want anyone else to know what was happening. But because I wasn't in New Jersey, I had to reach out to relatives to help by visiting and checking on him.

Then one day I received a call from the hospital asking me to come as soon as possible because my father might not have much time left. Not even ten seconds into the conversation, I heard emergency alarms sounding through the phone.

The doctor said franticly, "Hold on… hold on please!" There was chaos in the background. And then the doctor returned to the phone and said the words that stopped time.

"Mr. Gordon… I'm sorry. We just lost your father." I was standing in the middle of my office while people walked past me smiling and greeting me. The world around me kept moving. But everything inside of me stopped.

Another loss in the wilderness.

With the help of many people, some family, some friends, and some strangers, I was able to buried my father without completely losing my mind.

That season broke me.

God stripped me of everything I thought I had control over. And He left me in the wilderness long enough to remind me that He was the only one I truly needed.

Looking back now, I realize I was walking through my own version of the story of Job. Everything Job loved was taken from him, yet he never stopped loving God. During my wilderness season, I began to hear God more clearly than ever before. I realized that God was preparing me for the very prayers I had been asking Him to answer.

I had prayed to become a stronger man in my family.
A pillar for the next generation.
A man who could live a long and prosperous life.
A man who had a deeper relationship with God than ever before.

But preparation requires testing.

You cannot receive something you are not prepared to handle. If you do, you will lose it just as quickly as you receive it. Sometimes we must first recognize that we are lost before we can truly be found.

That is just what this devotional book is about. This devotional book was written while in my wilderness. It was written through tears. Through prayers. Through questions I didn't have answers to.

In this season I met incredible people, learned life-changing lessons, made mistakes, experienced breakthroughs, and discovered parts of myself I never knew existed. I experienced real love. Lost real love. And began to truly become the reflection of pure love.

Every devotional in this book was written during moments when I was searching for God and finding Him. Moments when I needed Him to find me. Moments when I was learning what it truly meant to surrender.

I prayed over these devotionals and asked God to allow this book to become a blessing for you who reads it. A guide to help prepare you for your next level and your next breakthrough.

Today, I am grateful.

Even for the losses.

My faith is stronger.
My vision is clearer.
My cup has been refilled and now it overflows in ways I never imagined.

And God has expanded my territory so that my overflow can bless others.

My prayer is that the same happens for you.

Because where you are right now is not where your story ends because...

Your location is not your destination.

God Bless,

SECTION I:

SEEING GOD DIFFERENTLY

(God's Nature & Wisdom)

GOD THINKS BIGGER THAN YOU DO

"No one will be able to stand against you as long as you live. For I will be with you as I was with Moses. I will not fail you or abandon you. "Be strong and courageous, for you are the one who will lead these people to possess all the land I swore to their ancestors I would give them. Be strong and very courageous. Be careful to obey all the instructions Moses gave you. Do not deviate from them, turning either to the right or to the left. Then you will be successful in everything you do. Study this Book of Instruction continually. Meditate on it day and night so you will be sure to obey everything written in it. Only then will you prosper and succeed in all you do. This is my command - be strong and courageous! Do not be afraid or discouraged. For the LORD your God is with you wherever you go." - Joshua 1:5-9

Scripture teaches that success in God's mission comes from following His lead and trusting His promises. When we refuse to follow His direction, our vision shrinks. He designed a kingdom yet we settle for a shack and become comfortable living in one. You living this way is a disrespect to God. We grow comfortable with survival when He intended expansion.

But when we surrender to His leadership, our sight changes. We begin to see beyond limitation. We see abundance. We see land we can steward, families we can nurture, and communities we are called to build and serve. God does not think small. He does not design small. And when we align with Him, our lives cannot remain small.

Staying on the straight path requires discipline. It requires devotion. We cannot afford to be distracted by people, opportunities, or applause that are not aligned with God's character or His promises. Not everything that glitters is purpose. Not everyone who claps is assigned.

We must walk with courage. Not arrogance but courage. Fear cannot lead us. Doubt cannot govern us. God is always present, and He does not abandon what He has placed His favor upon. What He ordains, He sustains.

But alignment is not casual. We must remain in His Word and become living expressions of it. God cannot only be around us; He must dwell within us.

Our speech should reflect His truth.
Our vision should mirror His heart.
Our decisions should echo His wisdom.

When God leads, the outcome is always greater than what we could have imagined on our own.

Because God thinks bigger than you and He invites you to think bigger with Him.

SCRIPTURE REMINDS US

Ephesians 3:2

"Now to Him who is able to do immeasurably more than all we ask or imagine, according to His power that is at work within us."

God doesn't just do more. He does immeasurably more. Beyond your strategy. Beyond your projections. Beyond your comfort zone. When we bond with God and his power, we can't even explain the magnitude of the work we completed or the results that no man could ever imagine.

Remember that out imagination is never the ceiling; it's the starting point of it all.

Jeremiah 29:11

"'For I know the plans I have for you,' declares the Lord, 'plans to prosper you and not to harm you, plans to give you hope and a future.'"

This scripture reinforces the intentional design. God's vision is never random. It is deliberate. It's divinely strategic. Structured. And forever forward-moving.

He sees the full blueprint when we only see the foundation.

REFLECTIONS

Where in my life have I settled for what feels safe instead of pursuing what God has shown me is possible?

What fears, distractions, or limiting beliefs are shrinking my vision below what God has promised? How can I destroy the shacks in my life and begin to move into the kingdom?

PRAYER

Heavenly Father, thank You for the vision and purpose You have placed over our lives. Forgive us for the times we settled for less when You called us to greater. Help us to surrender fully to Your leadership so that our lives align with Your will and not our limitations.

Give us discipline to stay on the path You have set before us. Guard our hearts from distractions, from opportunities that are not assigned to us, and from voices that pull us away from Your truth. Fill us with courage to move forward in faith, trusting that what You ordain, You will sustain.

Expand our vision to see what You see. Let our thoughts reflect Your wisdom, our words reflect Your truth, and our actions reflect Your purpose. May Your power work within us so that our lives produce more than we could ever ask or imagine. Amen.

PERSONAL DEVOTIONAL WRITING

GOD IS IN THE SILENCE OF QUIETNESS

"And to aspire to live quietly, and to mind your own affairs, and to work with your hands, as we instructed you, so that you may walk properly before outsiders and be dependent on no one."- 1 Thessalonians 4:11

To be quiet is to move in the frequency of God. We live in a world filled with constant noise, opinions, social media, endless commentary, and the pressure to always be visible. Yet Scripture teaches a powerful spiritual principle: God often speaks most clearly in quietness.

To live quietly does not mean to live passively or without purpose. Instead, it means to operate with discipline, humility, and focus, prioritizing your relationship with God above the distractions of the world. Silence creates space for clarity. When we remove ourselves from unnecessary noise, gossip, and constant comparison, we position ourselves to hear God's direction more clearly.

Quietness is a spiritual strategy. Many people seek influence by speaking loudly, promoting themselves constantly, or chasing attention. But throughout Scripture, God consistently works through those who develop their character in private before being elevated in public.

Operating in quietness keeps our focus where it belongs, on our work, our calling, and our relationship with God. When we mind our responsibilities and walk faithfully, our lives begin to speak louder than our words ever could.

One powerful example is the story of the prophet Elijah. After experiencing great victory, Elijah found himself exhausted and discouraged. As he waited on God, a mighty wind came, then an earthquake, and then a fire. But God was not in any of those dramatic displays.

"After the fire came a gentle whisper."- 1 Kings 19:12

God chose to speak to Elijah through a quiet whisper rather than through the noise of powerful events. This moment reminds us that God's voice is often found not in chaos, but in stillness.

Consider a professional who feels constant pressure to keep up with every conversation, trend, and controversy at work or online. Instead of joining the noise, they make a different choice. They focus on their responsibilities, continue developing their skills, maintain integrity, and spend time in prayer and reflection.

While others compete for attention, their quiet consistency begins to stand out. Their work ethic, wisdom, and calm leadership eventually earn them trust, respect, and opportunity. What looked like silence was actually preparation and positioning. And God often elevates those who are faithful in quiet seasons.

SCRIPTURE REMINDS US

Psalm 46:10

"Be still, and know that I am God."

Isaiah 30:15

"In repentance and rest is your salvation, in quietness and trust is your strength."

PRAYER

Heavenly Father, thank You for reminding me that Your presence is often found in stillness and quietness. Help me to step away from unnecessary noise and distractions so I can hear Your voice more clearly. Teach me to focus on the work and responsibilities You have given me while seeking Your approval above all else. Strengthen my discipline to walk humbly, live wisely, and trust that You are working even in the quiet seasons of my life. May my actions reflect Your wisdom and bring honor to Your name. In Jesus' name, Amen.

DON'T UNDERESTIMATE CONVERSATIONS WITH GOD

"Keep on asking, and you will receive what you ask for. Keep on seeking, and you will find. Keep on knockin, and the door will be opened to you. For everyone who asks, receives. Everyone who seeks, finds. And everyone who knocks, the door will be opened." – Matthew 7:7-8

It's easy to underestimate the power of simply talking to God. Life can be loud with deadlines, responsibilities, and challenges but God is waiting for us to bring Him our questions, needs, and desires. In moments of doubt, we sometimes think, "He probably won't hear me," or "It's too small to matter." Yet, scripture reminds us that asking, seeking, and knocking are not just rituals, they are expressions of faith.

Consider the story of Hannah in 1 Samuel 1. She poured out her heart in prayer for a child, even when others underestimated her grief and her requests seemed impossible. God responded in His perfect timing, blessing her with Samuel, who would become a prophet. Hannah's persistence reminds us that God is never too busy to listen, and His timing is always right, even when it feels delayed.

Imagine an entrepreneur, overwhelmed by the demands of a growing business. They spend sleepless nights worried about finances and staffing, thinking prayer alone won't solve tangible problems. Yet, when they pause, genuinely seek God's wisdom, and knock on the doors of opportunity with faith, guidance comes: a mentor appears, a new client comes through, or a solution emerges in an unexpected way. Just as with Hannah, the key is persistence, trust, and recognizing that God's timing, not our own, is perfect.

When you underestimate conversations with God, you risk missing divine guidance, favor, and breakthroughs that could change your life.

Prayer isn't just a spiritual exercise, it's a direct line to the One who orchestrates your entire life.

SCRIPTURES REMIND US

Jeremiah 33:3

"Call to Me and I will answer you and show you great and mighty things which you do not know."

Psalm 37:7

"Be still before the Lord and wait patiently for Him; do not fret when men succeed in their ways, when they carry out their wicked schemes."

REFLECTIONS

Are there areas in your life where you've stopped asking or seeking God because you felt your prayers were "too small" or insignificant?

How can you remind yourself to trust God's timing rather than trying to force solutions on your own?

PRAYER

Heavenly Father, thank you for always being ready to listen and guide me. Help me never to underestimate the power of my conversations with You. Teach me to ask boldly, seek earnestly, and knock persistently, trusting that Your timing is perfect. Give me patience in waiting, wisdom in listening, and faith to act when You open the doors. May I remember that no prayer is too small, no request too simple, and no timing too late for You, Lord. Amen.

PERSONAL DEVOTIONAL WRITING

GOD IS STRATEGIC, DON'T ATTACK WITHOUT HIM

"But the Lord told me to tell you, 'Do not attack, for I am not with you. If you go ahead on your own, you will be crushed by your enemies." – *Deuteronomy 1:42*

Bold moves are often necessary in life, whether in business, relationships, or personal growth. But God's Word reminds us that moving without His guidance can lead to unnecessary hardship, confusion, or defeat. In Deuteronomy 1:42, the Israelites attempted to enter the Promised Land without waiting for God's direction. Their impatience and failure to follow His strategy led to fear, rebellion, and consequences that could have been avoided.

God is a strategic God. He doesn't just give commands; He gives tactics, timing, and wisdom. Our role is to seek His counsel in prayer and solitude, listening carefully to the Holy Spirit before we make any significant moves. When we rush ahead without His confirmation, we risk stepping into situations that cause unnecessary struggle or loss.

Consider the story of Nehemiah (Nehemiah 2). When he saw Jerusalem's walls in ruins, he didn't immediately launch a reconstruction plan. Instead, he prayed, fasted, and sought God's favor before approaching the king. God's guidance allowed him to move with confidence, strategy, and provision, leading to a successful rebuilding of the city. Nehemiah's story is a blueprint for us: bold moves without God can fail; bold moves with God bring victory.

Imagine someone eager to launch a new business venture. They feel ready to move, the timing seems right, and the opportunity looks promising. But instead of seeking God's wisdom, they rush forward, only to encounter unexpected financial, legal, or logistical challenges. Had they paused in prayer, sought guidance, and waited for confirmation from the Holy Spirit, their bold move could have been timed for maximum impact, avoiding unnecessary pitfalls.

Whether you're confronting a challenge, pursuing a goal, or facing a situation that tests your patience, don't attack without God. His strategy will always outperform your plans. Move only when He signals it's time. Waiting may feel slow, but His timing guarantees success.

SCRIPTURE REMINDS US

Proverbs 3:5-6

"Trust in the Lord with all your heart, and do not lean on your own understanding. In all your ways acknowledge Him, and He will make your paths straight."

James 1:5

"If any of you lacks wisdom, let him ask of God, who gives to all liberally and without reproach, and it will be given to him."

REFLECTION

Are there areas of your life where you've moved without seeking God's guidance? What were the results?

How can you cultivate the habit of consulting God before making bold decisions or taking significant action?

PRAYER

Heavenly Father, thank you for being a God of strategy, wisdom, and perfect timing. Forgive me for the times I've acted impulsively without seeking Your guidance. Teach me to wait on You, to pray, and to listen for the promptings of Your Holy Spirit before I make bold moves. Give me clarity, courage, and the wisdom to act according to Your plan. Let my steps align with Your strategy so that every action I take brings success and honor to You. Amen.

ONLY GOD KNOWS WHY HE CHOSE YOU

"You didn't choose me. I chose you. I appointed you to go and produce lasting fruit, so that the father will give you whatever you ask for, using my name." - John 15:16

There's something powerful in realizing that God made the first move in choosing you. He didn't wait for you to prove your worthiness; He called you because He saw purpose, potential, and a plan in your life that only He could orchestrate. John 15:16 reminds us that our calling is intentional, and our lives have significance beyond what we can see.

Consider the story of Joseph (Genesis 37–50). God chose Joseph despite him being the youngest son, the dreamer, and seemingly the least likely to influence the course of nations. Joseph faced betrayal, slavery, and imprisonment, yet he remained aligned with God's purposes. In the end, God used him to save entire nations from famine. Joseph's fruitfulness wasn't a result of his own striving alone—it was a result of working smartly within God's plan and trusting the calling He had placed on his life.

Think about an entrepreneur, artist, or leader who was given a unique talent or opportunity that others might overlook. They could choose to work just hard, or they could work aligned with God's guidance, seeking wisdom and integrity in their decisions. When their efforts honor God, they produce lasting results, businesses thrive ethically, communities are positively impacted, and their work becomes a source of blessing for others. But when actions are out of alignment with God's plan, challenges multiply, and success is fleeting. Being chosen by God means you're part of something greater. Your life is meant to bear fruit that lasts. But fruitfulness requires alignment with Him, smart work, and obedience. The question isn't why you were chosen, that's God's secret, but how you will respond to His call.

SCRIPTURES REMINDS US

Ephesians 2:10

"For we are God's handiwork, created in Christ Jesus to do good works, which God prepared in advance for us to do."

Colossians 3:23-24

"Whatever you do, work at it with all your heart, as working for the Lord, not for human masters, since you know that you will receive an inheritance from the Lord as a reward. It is the Lord Christ you are serving."

REFLECTION

Are there areas in your life where you are trying to produce results without seeking alignment with God's calling?

How can you ensure that the work you do honors God and produces lasting fruit?

PRAYER

Heavenly Father, thank you for choosing me, even when I may not understand why. Help me to honor the calling You've placed on my life by aligning my actions, decisions, and work with Your purpose. Teach me to bear fruit that lasts and to rely on Your wisdom rather than my own understanding. May everything I produce bring glory to You, reflect Your love, and bless those around me. Keep me humble, focused, and faithful to the calling only You could place on my life. Amen.

PERSONAL DEVOTIONAL WRITING

GOD SEES THE END FROM THE BEGINNING

"I knew you before I formed you in your mother's womb. Before you were born, I set you apart and appointed you as my prophet to the nations." O Sovereign Lord," I said, "I can't speak for you! I'm too young!" The Lord replied, "Don't say, 'I'm too young,' for you must go wherever I send you and say whatever I tell you. [8] *And don't be afraid of the people, for I will be with you and will protect you. I, the Lord, have spoken!" Then the Lord reached out and touched my mouth and said, "Look, I have put my words in your mouth! Today I appoint you to stand up against nations and kingdoms. Some you must uproot and tear down, destroy and overthrow. Others you must build up and plant." - Jeremiah 1:5-10*

Every step you take has already been seen by God. Long before you recognized the opportunity, God had already prepared the moment. Nothing that unfolds in your life surprises Him. He goes before you, arranging circumstances, opening doors, and positioning you exactly where you need to be.

God does not measure readiness the way the world does. He does not choose based on age, title, education, height, or status. Time and time again, He selects the person who believes they are the least qualified. The one who thinks they are not ready to fight their Goliath, lead organizations, build wealth for their family, or step into positions they never formally trained for. Yet those are often the very people God appoints.

Why? Because His power is revealed most clearly through obedience and faith, not credentials.

You must remind yourself that you were created in God's light, love, and excellence. When He places a crown of responsibility on your life, it is not something to fear. It is something to steward. If God has called you to walk into a room, take a position, break a generational cycle, or lead where no one in your family has led before, it means He has already equipped you for it.

Human standards can feel intimidating. Job descriptions, qualifications, and expectations created by people may attempt to convince you that you are not ready. But what God has assigned to you cannot be taken by anyone else. When the opportunity appears, it is not accidental. It is confirmation.

Speak with authority, not arrogance. Walk with confidence, not pride. Ask God daily to guide your speech and your steps so that your leadership reflects His wisdom and His character.

The responsibility of God's calling is serious. When God appoints someone to uproot, rebuild, lead, or correct what is broken, it requires courage. Sometimes that courage must show up in your family. Sometimes it shows up in your workplace, your community, or your business. God often chooses unexpected people and uses unconventional methods to bring His vision to life.

Remember this: God sees the end from the beginning. The same God who designed the outcome also designed the person who would carry it out.

That person may very well be you.

SCRIPTURE REMINDS US

1 Corinthians 1:27

"But God chose the foolish things of the world to shame the wise; God chose the weak things of the world to shame the strong."

God intentionally chooses people the world overlooks so that His power, not human ability, can receive the glory.

1 Samuel 16:7

"For the Lord does not look at the things man looks at. A man looks at the outside of a person, but the Lord looks at the heart."

God dwell within and He chooses those that always has the best intention in heart and mind to do His will.

REFLECTIONS

Where in your life might God be calling you to step into something bigger than what you currently believe you are qualified for?

Are there fears, labels, or human standards that are causing you to hesitate in areas where God may already be opening doors

PRAYER

Heavenly Father, thank You for knowing my path before I ever took my first step. Help me trust the plans You have already prepared for my life. When opportunities appear that seem bigger than my experience or qualifications, remind me that You are the One who called me.

Remove fear, doubt, and hesitation from my heart. Strengthen my faith so I can walk boldly in the assignments You place before me. Guide my words, my decisions, and my leadership so that everything I do reflects Your wisdom and Your purpose.

Give me courage to break cycles, build what You have called me to build, and stand firm wherever You place me. Let my life be a reflection of Your power and Your plan. Amen.

PERSONAL DEVOTIONAL WRITING

LIVE DIFFERENTLY WITH GOD

"Yet, I am confident I will see the Lord's goodness while I am here in the land of the living. Wait patiently for the Lord. Be brave and courageous. Yes, wait patiently for the Lord." – Psalm 27:13-14

Living differently with God means embracing a life of patience, faith, and trust, even when circumstances feel stagnant or uncertain. The "land of the living" refers to this life, our present moment. It reminds us that while we are here, God's goodness is at work, even when we cannot see it immediately.

Waiting on God is rarely easy. There are times when it feels like our prayers are unheard, doors remain closed, or blessings are delayed. Yet, scripture assures us that God is a fulfilling God, and He is always in control. He moves mountains, parts seas, and orchestrates circumstances far beyond our own capability. Our task is to practice patience, exercise faith, and trust the process.

A biblical example of this is Moses (Exodus 3–14). Moses spent decades preparing before God used him to lead the Israelites out of Egypt. He faced long periods of waiting, self-doubt, and seemingly impossible circumstances. But God's timing was perfect. When Moses finally acted, he witnessed miracles such as the Red Sea parted, and freedom was achieved. Moses' life demonstrates that transformation and readiness happen in the waiting, not just in the action.

Consider an individual seeking a career breakthrough or personal milestone. They may feel frustrated as opportunities seem delayed. Living differently with God means using that waiting period to grow in learning skills, developing character, and preparing spiritually and mentally. When the timing is right, the breakthrough arrives with greater impact, just as God intended. Rushing the process often leads to missed lessons, stress, and setbacks.

Living differently with God is choosing faith over fear, patience over impatience, and preparation over frustration. It is being present in the moment, trusting that God is perfecting your life, lessons, and character before opening doors and answering prayers.

SCRIPTURES REMINDS US

Isaiah 40:31

"But those who wait on the Lord shall renew their strength; they shall mount up with wings like eagles, they shall run and not be weary, they shall walk and not faint."

James 1:4

"Let perseverance finish its work so that you may be mature and complete, not lacking anything."

REFLECTION

Are there areas of your life where impatience has caused you to act before God's timing?

How can you use the waiting period to grow spiritually, mentally, and emotionally while trusting God's plan?

PRAYER

Heavenly Father, thank you for Your faithfulness, even when I cannot see immediate results. Teach me to live differently with You—exercising patience, faith, and trust in Your perfect timing. Help me focus on transformation, wisdom, and lessons in this season, knowing that You are preparing me for what is to come. Strengthen my heart, renew my spirit, and remind me to be present in the land of the living, trusting that Your goodness will be revealed at the right time. Amen.

PERSONAL DEVOTIONAL WRITING

THE SPIRIT
IN THE WORD

"In the beginning was the Word, and the Word was with God, and the Word was God. He was in the beginning with God. All things were made through him, and without him was not any thing made that was made." - John 1:1-3

God cannot be contained in a box, a theory, or a human explanation. No academic degree, philosophy, or intellectual framework can fully capture who He is. Scripture reminds us that God is the Author of everything, the One who existed before time, space, and creation itself. John 1:1–3 teaches that the Word was with God and was God, and through Him all things were created.

The Word represents both God's voice and His Spirit in action. When God speaks, creation happens. When His Word moves, the impossible becomes possible.

Human beings often try to measure God using logic, science, or philosophy. But God transcends every measurement system humanity has created. His miracles cannot be predicted. His power cannot be weighed. His movement cannot be controlled. His blessings cannot be scheduled by human calendars.

When you look at the world around you the stars in the sky, the oceans in motion, the precision of life itself, it becomes clear that all creation reflects the vision of a Creator far beyond human comprehension. Everything that exists was first spoken into existence by God.

But God does something even more remarkable: He chooses people to participate in His vision. Throughout history, God has used ordinary individuals to bring His divine plans into reality.

A powerful biblical example is Bezalel, the craftsman chosen by God to build the Tabernacle (Exodus 31:1–5). God filled him with the Spirit of wisdom, understanding, and skill to create sacred objects for worship. Bezalel didn't invent the vision; God gave it to him. His role was to bring God's design into the physical world. This shows how the Spirit in the Word works: God speaks the vision, and people are empowered to build it.

In modern life, this principle still operates. Think about innovators, creators, leaders, and builders who develop ideas that transform industries, communities, or culture. Behind many of those visions is a divine spark—an inspiration that did not originate purely from human thinking. When people align themselves with God's purpose, He often gives them ideas, wisdom, and direction to create something meaningful that blesses others.

The world we see today is filled with things that began as a thought inspired by God and spoken into action. Every invention, business, movement, or piece of art that blesses humanity reflects this principle: God provides the vision, and people bring it into reality through obedience and faith.

Understanding this truth should humble us. Our role is not to control God's plans but to listen for His Word and allow His Spirit to guide us. When we align with His vision, our work becomes more than effort—it becomes participation in God's creative purpose.

You were created intentionally. God has a plan for your life that fits into His larger design. The same God who spoke the universe into existence is capable of speaking purpose into your life and guiding you to build something meaningful in this world.

SCRIPTURES REMIND US

Colossians 1:16–17

"For in Him all things were created: things in heaven and on earth, visible and invisible… all things have been created through Him and for Him. He is before all things, and in Him all things hold together."

Isaiah 55:8–9

"For My thoughts are not your thoughts, neither are your ways My ways," declares the Lord. "As the heavens are higher than the earth, so are My ways higher than your ways and My thoughts than your thoughts."

REFLECTIONSS

How can you create space in your life to hear God's voice and align your actions with His vision?

What gifts, talents, or ideas might God be placing in your life to bring His purposes into reality?

PRAYER

Heavenly Father, you are the Creator of all things and the source of every good idea, vision, and purpose. Your wisdom is beyond human understanding, and Your power cannot be measured. Thank You for allowing us to participate in the plans You have designed for this world.

Help me to quiet my mind so that I can hear Your Word and follow the leading of Your Spirit. Teach me to trust that Your plans are greater than my own and that Your timing is perfect. Give me the wisdom to recognize the ideas and opportunities You place before me and the courage to act faithfully when You call.

May the work of my hands reflect Your vision and bring glory to Your name. Use my life as a vessel to build what You desire in this world. Amen.

PERSONAL DEVOTIONAL WRITING

SECTION II:

TRUSTING GOD IN THE PROCESS

(Waiting, Stretching, Becoming)

FAITH
& ENDURANCE

"I can do all things through him who strenghtens me." -Phillipians 4:13

There was a day when I had nothing to write about. I was dealing with everything all at once, and I couldn't gather my thoughts enough to put anything on the page. All I could do was turn to Scripture, seeking encouragement and endurance to keep pushing forward when nothing seemed to connect, click,
or come together.

So, I found a few scriptures that spoke directly to my spirit, and I wrote them out by hand. I pray these same scriptures give you the fulfillment they gave me, the strength to keep moving forward when everything feels low, exhaustion sets in, or hope seems distant.

Keep the faith and endure, for your best is yet to come, my brothers and sisters.

"Dear brothers and sisters, when troubles of any kind come your way, consider it an opportunity for great joy. For you know that when your faith is tested, your endurance has a chance to grow. So let it grow, for when your endurance is fully developed, you will be perfect and complete, needing nothing.

If you need wisdom, ask our generous God, and he will give it to you. He will not rebuke you for asking. But when you ask him, be sure that your faith is in God alone. Do not waver, for a person with divided loyalty is as unsettled as a wave of the sea that is blown and tossed by the wind. Such people should not expect to receive anything from the Lord. Their loyalty is divided between God and the world, and they are unstable in everything they do.

Believers who are poor have something to boast about, for God has honored them. And those who are rich should boast that God has humbled them. They will fade away like a little flower in the field. The hot sun rises and the grass withers; the little flower droops and falls, and its beauty fades away. In the same way, the rich will fade away with all of their achievements.

God blesses those who patiently endure testing and temptation. Afterward they will receive the crown of life that God has promised to those who love him. And remember, when you are being tempted, do not say, "God is tempting me." God is never tempted to do wrong, and he never tempts anyone else. Temptation comes from our own desires, which entice us and drag us away. These desires give birth to sinful actions. And when sin is allowed to grow, it gives birth to death.

So don't be misled, my dear brothers and sisters. Whatever is good and perfect is a gift coming down to us from God our Father, who created all the lights in the heavens. He never changes or casts a shifting shadow. He chose to give birth to us by giving us his true word. And we, out of all creation, became his prized possession.

Understand this, my dear brothers and sisters: You must all be quick to listen, slow to speak, and slow to get angry. Human anger does not produce the righteousness God desires. So get rid of all the filth and evil in your lives, and humbly accept the word God has planted in your hearts, for it has the power to save your souls.

But don't just listen to God's word. You must do what it says. Otherwise, you are only fooling yourselves. For if you listen to the word and don't obey, it is like glancing at your face in a mirror. You see yourself, walk away, and forget what you look like. But if you look carefully into the perfect law that sets you free, and if you do what it says and don't forget what you heard, then God will bless you for
doing it.

If you claim to be religious but don't control your tongue, you are fooling yourself, and your religion is worthless. Pure and genuine religion in the sight of God the Father means caring for orphans and widows in their distress and refusing to let the world corrupt you." – James 1:2-27

"May the God of hope fill you with all joy and peace in believing, so that by the power of the Holy Spirit you may abound in hope." – Romans 5:13

"And we know that for those who love God all things work together for

good, for those who are called according to his purpose." – Romans 8:28

"But he said to me, "My grace is sufficient for you, for my power, is made perfect in weakness." Therefore I will boost all more gladly of my weakness, so that the power of Christ may rest upon me." – 2 Corinthians 12:9

"Patient endurance is what you need now, so that you will continue to do God's will. Then you will receive all that he has promised." - Hebrews 10:36

"I have told you these things, so that in me you may have peace. In this world you will have trouble. But take heart! I have overcome the world." – John 16:33

"Beloved, do not believe every spirit, but test the spirits to see whether they are from God, for many false prophets have gone out into the world." - 1 John 4:1

"Submit yourself therefore to God. Resist the devil, and he will flee from you." - James 4:7

"I am the Lord who opened a way through the waters, making a dry path through the sea." – Isaiah 43:16

(God reminds us in this specific scripture that He can make a way out of no way. He always has and He always will. Where there is a sea of doubt or deep troubles, He will prove to us that there is still a clear path even if we don't see it.)

PERSONAL DEVOTIONAL WRITING

BE FLUENT IN PRAYER AND POSTURE

"Be anxious for nothing but in everything by prayer and supplication, with thanksgiving let your requests be made known to God; and the peace of God, which surpasses all understanding, will guard your heart and mind s through Christ Jesus." - Philippian 4:6-7

Don't force or move to fast towards or for something that isn't ready for you (or not actually yours). We should ask in prayer and have patience with God. We should talk in prayer language which is God's language. If we are fluent in this language, we will begin to understand clearly where we need to be, at the appropriate time, and in what energy. Be peaceful always. Be patient always. Be in divine connection always.

"Once you realize the power of the tongue, you won't just say anything. Once you realize the power of your thoughts, you won't just entertain anything. Once you find out the power of your presence, you won't just be anywhere." - Unknown

This also goes for your energy. Once you know the power of energy, you won't just share it with anyone.

In Mark 9:23, Jesus says, "*What do you mean, 'If I can?' ... Anything is possible if a person believes.*" This statement reveals the power of belief with confidence. Trust, confidence, and faith are some of the central themes throughout the Bible. They must become our unwavering attitudes if we desire to see God perform wonders in our lives and in the lives of others.

Faith is not wishful thinking; it is confident trust in who God is and what He is able to do. But prayer plays a vital role in activating that faith. No matter how strong our belief may be, we still depend entirely on God to bring the outcome. Faith positions us but God produces the result.

Our faith becomes the key that unlocks the door to blessing. It aligns our hearts with heaven's authority. When we trust fully without doubt or hesitation, we demonstrate that we believe God is both willing and able.

Trust Him. Have faith in Him. Know that He is the foundation upon which your belief stands. And when your belief is rooted in Him, miracles are no longer distant possibilities. They become divine realities in His perfect timing.

SCRIPTURE REMINDS US

Hebrews 11:6

"And without faith it is impossible to please God, because anyone who comes to Him must believe that He exists and that He rewards those who earnestly seek Him."

This reinforces that belief is not optional, it is foundational. Faith is what positions us to receive from God.

James 1:6–7

"But when you ask, you must believe and not doubt, because the one who doubts is like a wave of the sea, blown and tossed by the wind. That person should not expect to receive anything from the Lord."

This reminds us that divided belief weakens expectation. Steady faith creates spiritual stability and confidence in God's provision

REFLECTIONS

Do I truly believe God is able to do what I am praying for, or am I praying with quiet doubt?

How does my confidence show up when I talk to myself and others about my beliefs?

PRAYER

Dear God,

My prayer is simple today. Help me to be extraordinary in my prayer life. May the words I speak be aligned with the language of the Spirit. Fix my posture so that it reflects royalty, confidence, humility, and divine authority.

May those who come into my presence recognize that You are within me at all times. Strengthen my faith so that it never wavers. Speak to me when I need to be still and speak clearly when it is time for me to move with power and authority.

Let my life reflect Your presence in every room I enter.
Amen.

BUILDING ON SOLID GROUND (FOUNDATION)

"Anyone who listens to my teaching and follows it is wise, like a person who builds a house on solid rock. Though the rain comes in torrents and the floodwaters rise and the winds beat against that house, it won't collapse because it is built on bedrock. But anyone who hears my teaching and doesn't obey it is foolish, like a person who builds a house on sand. When the rains and floods come and the winds beat against that house, it will collapse with a mighty crash." - Matthew 7: 24-27

We must establish a strong foundation so that no matter the season, we do not lose ourselves to the winds of life. When we are not living rightly, anyone or anything can take whatever the amount we might have. We will be tested constantly, fighting internal and external battles at the same time. That is why we must be equipped and our roots planted firmly in God.

We cannot live "on the fence" with our decisions. We must be firm, direct, and fully sold on our vision, steady in our speech, disciplined in our actions, intentional in our relationships, and unwavering in our roots in God.

My spiritual mother, who is also a minister, once spoke to me about the anointing over my life and over the lives of many others. She said we must not allow others to shift or weaken our foundation. We do not need a co-signer for what God directly placed within us…especially when He was clear and intentional about our assignment.

If your foundation is weak, strengthen it.

Nothing stands on shaky ground. Nothing lasting is built on instability. Everything can endure the weather of life and the winds of change when the foundation is set properly. Families flourish when their structure rests on a solid foundation. This can be in the form of healthy traditions, love, communication, respect, and above all, clarity of vision.

Foundations are formed when the builder has a clear plan. Clear instructions ensure that everyone understands their role, their position, and the gifts they are called to use.

And we must never forget the wisdom of those who came before us, our elders. They have seen floods. They have endured storms. They have watched seasons change again and again over decades. Why wouldn't we lean on them as we build, expand, and protect what we've been given?

They are part of our bedrock.
They are steady because they have been tested.
They speak to God in ways we aspire to.

And if we listen, truly listen, we will learn how to stand when the winds begin to blow.

SCRIPTURE REMINDS US

Proverbs 3:5–6

"Trust in the Lord with all your heart; do not depend on your own understanding. Seek His will in all you do, and He will show you which path to take."

Trust sounds simple until control is taken off the table. We often say we trust God, but what we really mean is we trust Him as long as the outcome matches our expectations.

This scripture challenges that.

It tells us not to lean on our own understanding. That means our logic, our experience, our degrees, our strategy, and even our past wins cannot be the ultimate authority in our lives. There will be moments when the vision doesn't make sense, when the timing feels off, and when the numbers don't add up. That is where faith becomes real.

Seeking His will in all we do requires daily alignment. Not occasional prayer. Not convenient obedience. Daily alignment.

When we truly surrender our need to control every step, clarity comes. Direction comes. Peace comes. Not because the road becomes easier but because we know Who is leading us.

Trust is not passive. It is active surrender.

And when we release our grip, God steadies our path.

"He is like a tree planted by streams of water, which yields its fruit in season and whose leaf does not wither - whatever they do prospers." - Psalm 1:3

This scripture reinforces rootedness. The strength isn't in the tree's appearance, it's in where it's planted. Placement determines endurance.

REFLECTIONS

What areas of my life am I building on sand? Where do I hear truth but fail to apply it?

What daily disciplines am I practicing that strengthen my spiritual foundation and where am I inconsistent?

PRAYER

Dear God, we come before You with humility and gratitude, acknowledging that You alone are the true foundation of our lives. Lord, anchor us deeply in You so that when the winds of life begin to blow, we will not be moved. Strengthen our roots so that we are not shaken by pressure, confusion, or the opinions of others.

Father, help us to live with integrity and alignment. Guard our hearts from compromise and from living "on the fence" in our decisions. Make us firm in our vision, steady in our words, disciplined in our actions, and intentional in our relationships. Give us the courage to stand fully in the assignments You have placed on our lives without needing validation from others. Remind us that what You have spoken over us is already established in heaven.

Lord, where our foundation has been weak, rebuild it. Where cracks have formed through doubt, fear, or distraction, repair them with Your wisdom and truth. Teach us to build our lives, our families, and our work on principles that will endure every season. Let love, clarity, respect, and purpose be the structure that holds everything together.

We thank You for the elders and mentors You have placed around us. Give us the humility to listen to their wisdom and the discernment to recognize the value of their experience. Help us learn from those who have endured storms and remained faithful through the seasons of life.

Father, teach us to trust You with all our hearts and not lean on our own understanding. Align our thoughts, our strategies, and our plans with Your will daily. When the path ahead does not make sense, remind us that Your guidance is greater than our logic and Your timing is perfect.

Plant us like trees by streams of living water. Nourish us through Your Word, strengthen us through Your Spirit, and allow us to bear fruit in every season. May our lives remain steady, prosperous in purpose, and unwavering in faith because our roots are firmly planted in You.

No matter what storms come, let us stand. Amen.

PERSONAL DEVOTIONAL WRITING

IN OUR JOB SEASON

"After you have suffered a little while, He will restore you and make you strong, firm and steadfast." - *1 Peter 5:10*

We will suffer and go through some very hard times and seasons within our lives. It is inevitable. I call this our Job Season. It's when we go through a chapter in our life when all seems lost. We are stripped naked from al the things we held in high esteem. Our relationship. Our Home. Our friendship. Our Finances. Our Health. Our Community. Our family. In our Job season, we are challenged in more ways than one. We are confused at times. We are shaken and questioning God as to why is this happening to me. I didn't deserve what is happening to me. Trust me, I'm old enough to experience these moments more than once. But in my walk now, I am fully aware that these are only moments. We may endure for a night, but joy comes in the morning. It may take many nights but our faith must t be strong enough to endure.

In our Job season, we are sometimes asked to strip down from all that we know. Isaiah 43:18 states, "Do not remember the former things, nor consider the things of the old." God puts us into this season because He wants us to be made new and not to rely or use what was. We must leave it all in the past. Our job season has us fastening out the old to create something new. It could be a new narrative of your life. Birth a new vision. Recognize another gift to unwrap. To become wiser in your walk. To mature and take responsibility for your family, village, and community. We have to walk differently when in this season because it slows us down to observe what we paid no attention to or was distracted to recognized. Once we start, we talk a different talk. Walk a different walk. You may become fully pregnant with a new vision, dream, and goal that has to be birth in your Job season.

Remember that God does His greatest work on us in the wilderness. Our Job season.

Our Job season is our own personal spiritual wilderness.

It's also an opportunity for transformation.

In our wilderness, we get to a point when we can't do anything but wait on God. When you are waiting on the Lord to provide direction or to hear his voice – meditate on His word and quiet any artificial noise. If you aren't hearing God's voice, just be still, and continue to be patience until you do. Be still with unwavering expectations. Keep the faith always in the wilderness during your Job season.

God puts us in seasons to season us better than we were before. The wilderness changes us. Builds us.

It is the most trying and hardest moment in our life that stretches us to strengthen us.

We will suffer. We will endure hard seasons. That is not optional, it is inevitable. I call this our *Job season*. It is the chapter of life when everything feels as though it is slipping through our hands.

We are stripped of the things we once held in high esteem - our relationships, our home, our friendships, our finances, our health, our community, and
our family.

In our Job season, we are challenged in more ways than one. We are confused. We are shaken. We find ourselves asking God, *Why is this happening to me? I didn't deserve this.*

I have lived long enough to experience these moments more than once. But now I understand something I didn't before: these are moments, not permanent identities.

Weeping may endure for a night, but joy comes in the morning. The night may feel long. It may even stretch across many sleepless nights. But it is still not forever. Our faith must be strong enough to endure the dark until the light breaks through.

In the Job season, we are often required to let go of what we once depended on. As Isaiah 43:18 says, "Do not remember the former things, nor consider the things of old." God does not lead us into this season to destroy us, but to renew us. He strips away what was so He can introduce what will be.

We must leave the past in the past. The Job season forces out the old to make room for the new.

It may birth a new narrative for your life.
It may awaken a vision you ignored.
It may reveal a gift you had not yet unwrapped.
It may mature you into the leader your family and community need.

This season slows us down. It forces us to observe what we once overlooked. It exposes distractions. It refines our focus. And as we begin to shift internally, our language changes. Our posture changes. Our decisions change.

You may even find yourself pregnant with a new vision - one that can only be developed in the wilderness before it is revealed in the open.

Because God does His most incredible work in the wilderness.

Our Job season is our personal spiritual wilderness.
It is uncomfortable.
It is uncertain.
But it is transformative.

There comes a point in this season (wilderness) when we can do nothing but wait on God. When direction feels silent and clarity seems delayed, that is not the time to panic -it is the time to be still.

Meditate on His Word.
Silence artificial noise.
Resist the urge to force outcomes.

If you do not hear His voice immediately, remain patient. Be still with expectation. Keep the faith in the wilderness.

God places us in seasons to season us. To strengthen what was fragile. To build what was undeveloped. To deepen what was shallow.

The wilderness changes us. It stretches us. And in stretching us, it strengthens us.

Your hardest season may become the birthplace of your strongest self.

In the Book of Job, Job did not lose something specific. He lost *everything*. When I say everything, I speaking of his wealth, children, health, and reputation. What makes his story powerful is not just the loss, but the silence of heaven above and the heaven surrounding him during it. Job did not get an immediate explanation. He did not receive a timeline. He just endured in his faith until he received the greatest endurance that was documented at the time.

Yet in Job 1:21, he says, *"The Lord gave, and the Lord has taken away; blessed be the name of the Lord."* That is not denial. That is anchored faith. Job teaches us that integrity in our suffering matters more than comfort in prosperity.

And you know what, the part we often rush past is that Job's latter days were greater than his former. Restoration came. Double came. But the doubling was not the reward, the refinement was.

Now look at Moses.

Moses had a calling on his life long before he recognized and understood it. And before he could lead a nation, he spent forty years in the wilderness. Not forty minutes. Not forty days. He spent forty long years. Tending sheep. Hidden. Forgotten by many. He went from being part of the royal family, living in a palace, having powerful political ties to living in complete desert obscurity.

That wilderness was not his punishment; it was his preparation. Just like yours.

The same man who once acted impulsively and killed an Egyptian had to be slowed down. The desert trained his temperament. The desert developed his dependence. The desert completely stripped his ego. It humbled him to his core.

Then, in the wilderness, God spoke through a burning bush.

Did you catch the similarity of both of their walk in the widernes?
Job lost everything before he saw restoration.

Moses wandered before he walked in assignment.

In both stories, suffering and wilderness were never detours. They were development stages.

They couldn't rush the season. They couldn't cut the process short. They had to walk through it.

Your Job season may feel like loss.
Your Moses moment may feel like delay.

But both are divine classrooms.

Like Job, you may not get immediate answers, but you can maintain faith.
Like Moses, you may feel hidden, but you are being shaped for something major.

The wilderness clarifies who you are without applause.
Loss reveals what you worship.
Delay reveals what you trust.

And here is the thread tying it together:

God does not waste wilderness.
God does not waste suffering.
God does not waste stripping seasons in your wilderness walk

Job came out refined.
Moses came out commissioned.

And you will come out stronger, wiser, and more aligned than when you entered.

SCRIPTURE REMINDS US

Exodus 3:12

"And God said, 'I will be with you. And this will be the sign to you that it is I who have sent you: When you have brought the people out of Egypt, you will worship God on this mountain.'"

Even in preparation and delay, God's presence and guidance are constant. The wilderness is not abandonment; it's refinement and readiness for assignment.

Job 13:15

"Though He slay me, yet will I hope in Him; I will surely defend my ways to His face."

We must always endure loss and confusion while maintaining faith. It's about trusting God even when circumstances are inexplicable. Where many will break, we build in this season. Where many will quit, we keep going in this season.

REFLECTIONS

What did you learn about yourself in your previous wilderness during your Job season? Looking back at this, what else can I see clearly that I didn't when I first came out of it?

What might God be developing in me currently through this wilderness that I would not have gained in a season of comfort or visibility?

THE POWER OF WISE COUNSEL

"He immediately consulted with his wise advisers, who knew all the Persian laws and customs, for he always asked for their advice." - Esther 1:13

Leadership is never a solo journey. Scripture reminds us that every effective leader surrounds themselves with a circle of wise advisors, individuals who understand the laws, customs, and nuances of the environment in which decisions are made. Whether you are an accountant, lawyer, business owner, educator, or public official, the principle holds: your effectiveness is amplified when you seek counsel from those who hold deep expertise and insight.

"Now the turn came for Esther, the daughter of Abihail, the brother of the father of Mordecai who had taken her as his daughter, to go in to the king. She did not ask for anything except what Hegai, the king's servant who took care of the women, said she should take. And Esther found favor in the eyes of all who saw her." Esther 2:1

Esther recognized that she did not have all the knowledge she needed about court life, the king's preferences, or palace protocol. So, she sought counsel from those closest to the source of power, women who knew the king intimately and had experience navigating the palace. Through their guidance, she positioned herself to make informed decisions that ultimately saved a nation.

The lesson is timeless: knowledge and wisdom are the most valuable currency in leadership. Decisions guided by insight from trusted advisors, not assumptions or pride, tend to succeed. Leaders who surround themselves with people who have direct experience, institutional memory, or unique expertise gain the advantage of perspective.

Historical Perspective on Wise Counsel:

- King Solomon famously asked for wisdom above riches or power, and he built a court of advisors and scribes to help govern Israel effectively (1 Kings 3:5–14).
- Ancient civilizations, from Egypt to Rome, emphasized councils of elders, senates, or advisory boards. The Roman Senate, for example, acted as an advisory body to guide the emperor in civil, military, and political matters, showing the enduring principle that wise counsel strengthens leadership.
- Confucian teachings highlight that the virtue of a leader lies not just in personal talent but in listening to ministers and advisers who understand the people and the systems under their care.

The principle is clear: no matter your position, the decisions you make today will be more effective when informed by those who know the terrain, understand the rules, and have direct insight from the source. Surround yourself with wisdom, and you will lead with confidence, clarity, and purpose.

SCRIPTURE REMINDS US

Proverbs 11:14

"Where there is no guidance, a people falls, but in an abundance of counselors there is safety."

This scripture emphasizes the safety, effectiveness, and foresight that come from seeking advice and multiple perspectives. Leaders who surround themselves with wise counsel are far more likely to succeed than those who rely solely on their own understanding.

Proverbs 15:22

"Plans fail for lack of counsel, but with many advisers they succeed."

This scripture reinforces the principle that informed decisions and strategic planning require insight from others. Wisdom from trusted advisors transforms ideas into actionable, successful outcomes.

REFLECTION

Who are the trusted advisors, mentors, or experts in my life whose guidance I actively seek before making important decisions?

Are there areas where I am relying on my own understanding instead of seeking insight from those with experience or direct knowledge of the situation?

How can I cultivate a culture of wisdom and counsel in my personal and professional life so that my decisions reflect clarity, knowledge, and foresight?

PRAYER

Heavenly Father,

Thank You for the wisdom demonstrated in the life of Esther and the leaders of history. Help me to surround myself with wise advisors who can provide insight, guidance, and understanding. Teach me humility to seek counsel when I do not know the path and discernment to recognize those whose advice aligns with Your will. May my decisions reflect knowledge, wisdom, and integrity, and may the counsel I receive guide me to lead effectively in every area of my life. Amen.

START OVER
TO GET OVER

"To everything there is a season, and a time to every purpose under heaven." - Ecclesiastes 3:1

Sometimes in life, you have to start over in order to truly get over what was meant only for a previous season of your life.

We often convince ourselves that we must hold on to certain people, habits, roles, or environments simply because of the time, energy, and emotion we invested in them. But God never intended every blessing, opportunity, or relationship to travel with us into every season.

I once heard a wise saying: *"It's better to choose change now than to be forced to change later by a situation or by someone else."* There is truth in that. Life has a way of pushing us forward when we resist the growth God is calling us into.

We have to keep in memory the acronym "B.L.L." – which stands for Building, Learning, and Letting Go.

- Some seasons are for building.
- Some seasons are for learning.
- Some seasons are for letting go.

The challenge for many of us is that we struggle to release what once mattered deeply to us. We remember the memories, the effort, and the history we built there. But new seasons require new investments of energy, new patterns, and new experiences.

Scripture teaches us that moving forward often requires leaving something behind:

"Forget the former things; do not dwell on the past. See, I am doing a new thing!" - Isaiah 43:18–19

This is why gratitude is so powerful.

Gratitude allows us to release without resentment.
Gratitude allows us to move forward without bitterness.
Gratitude reminds us that every person, place, and experience played a role in shaping who we are today.

Just because we release something does not mean we no longer appreciate it.

The Apostle Paul described spiritual growth this way:

"When I was a child, I spoke like a child, I thought like a child, I reasoned like a child. When I became a man, I put away childish things." - 1 Corinthians 13:11

Growth requires transition. Transition requires courage.

As many of you step into a new season of life, take small steps forward with gratitude. Thank God for the people, places, and experiences that helped shape your journey.

And as you release them, make room for the new opportunities, relationships, wisdom, and responsibilities that will help sustain you in the season ahead.

SCRIPTURE REMINDS US

1 Thessalonians 5:18

"Be thankful in all circumstances; for this is God's will for you."

No matter what is happening in our lives and around us, we must give thanks. All things work for the greater good of God's glory. He knows and sees all. So, we must be thankful in our faith that God will make all things clear for us in the new seasons that arise.

2 Corinthians 5:17

"Therefore, if anyone is in Christ, the new creation has come: The old has gone, the new is here!"

This scripture reminds us that when God is doing something new in our lives, He is not adding to what is current or old - He is transforming us completely. Everything will be made new. Which will make us unrecognizable. Sometimes stepping into the new requires releasing the former version of ourselves, our past environments, and even past mindsets so we can fully walk in what God is creating now.

REFLECTIONS

What is something from a previous season of my life that God may be asking me to release so I can fully embrace the new season He is leading me into?

How can I practice gratitude for my past experiences while still having the faith and courage to move forward into what God is doing next in my life?

PRAYER

I come before You today with faith, joy, and a heart full of gratitude. As I step into the new season You are leading me into, I ask that You grant me wisdom and strength. Show me clearly what and who I must release so that I can fully walk in the purpose You have prepared for me.

I recognize that I have invested time, energy, and resources into many things during seasons that may now be coming to an end. Lord, prepare my heart for these transitions. Renew me in every area of my life - my mind, my spirit, my habits, and my direction.

I desire to honor You in all that I do. Help me to faithfully surrender the small things each day that no longer serve Your will for my life, so that I may serve You more fully and walk more closely in Your purpose.

I thank You in advance for Your guidance, Your provision, and Your grace as You continue to shape my path.

Amen.

I DON'T CHASE, I ATTRACT

"Do not be anxious about anything, but in every situation, by prayer and petition, with thanksgiving, present your requests to God. And the peace of God, which transcends all understanding, will guard your hearts and your minds in Christ Jesus." - Philippian 4:6-7

Don't force or rush toward something that isn't ready for you or isn't truly yours. Instead, ask in prayer and practice patience with God. Speak in the language of prayer, God's language. When we become fluent in this language, we begin to clearly understand where we need to be, at the right time, and in the right energy.

Be peaceful. Be patient. Remain in divine connection. There is no need to rush or be anxious. What belongs to you will naturally come to you in its perfect timing.

I once heard this: Once you realize the power of your words, you won't say just anything. Once you understand the power of your thoughts, you won't entertain just anything. Once you grasp the power of your presence, you won't be just anywhere. Once you know the power of your energy, you won't share it with just anyone. And once you know the power of God, you won't rush or fear anything.

Suppose you're waiting for a career opportunity or a relationship to align with your life. Instead of forcing outcomes, pray for guidance, remain patient, and observe the signs God places before you. By staying centered and connected, you'll recognize the right moment and approach. And your energy will naturally attract what is truly meant for you.

SCRIPTURE REMINDS US

Ecclesiastes 3:1

"There is a time for everything, and a season for every activity under the heavens."

Isaiah 40:31

"But those who hope in the Lord will renew their strength. They will soar on wings like eagles; they will run and not grow weary, they will walk and not be faint."

REFLECTION

In what areas of my life am I trying to force outcomes instead of waiting on God's timing?

How can I practice speaking, thinking, and acting in alignment with God's energy today?

PRAYER

Father, help me to trust Your timing. Teach me to speak, think, and act in alignment with Your will. Remove my anxiety and impatience, and help me to remain connected to Your peace and guidance. Let me recognize the opportunities that are truly meant for me, and give me the patience to wait for them in faith. Amen.

GOD WORKS BEST IN THE CUT

"Fear not, for I am with you; Be not dismayed, for I am your God. I will strengthen you, Yes, I will help you, I will uphold you with my righteous hand." - Isaiah 41:10

Scripture reminds us that we have nothing to fear when we trust that God is with us. If we believe He has helped us in the past and continues to be present, why do we allow fear to take hold? Why do we worry that the sacrifices we've made or the work we've poured into our lives will not yield the results we hope for?

Fear often creeps in during moments of weakness or uncertainty. When we cannot see the full picture or know the timing of God's intervention, doubt can arise. But it is precisely in these moments that faith must take the lead. We lean on the promises of Scripture, recall past experiences of God's faithfulness, and trust that He will come through at the perfect time just as He always has. The unknown may feel intimidating, but God's hand is always holding us, guiding us, and strengthening us.

Think of your life as a diamond in the making. Diamonds are not born perfect. They are raw, uncut, and often imperfect in appearance at first. But God is the jeweler to our lives, and He know how to make sure the 3 C's are perfect once He gets done with us.

Cut: The "cut" of a diamond determines how it reflects light and reveals its brilliance. Similarly, the challenges, trials, and uncertainties in your life are the cutting process God uses to shape your character and refine your faith.

Clarity: Diamonds must be cleaned and polished to reveal their full beauty. Moments of fear, doubt, or weakness are like polishing. God uses these times to refine your perspective and prepare you for the fullness of His plan.

Carat: A diamond's weight reflects its value. Your perseverance, faith, and trust in God increase your spiritual "weight" and the impact of your life for His glory.

Like a diamond, your full brilliance is revealed only after enduring pressure, cuts, and polishing. Fear not the unknown or the timing of God's intervention because these are part of the process of refinement. Trust that God is actively shaping and strengthening you, and your life will shine with unmatched radiance in His perfect timing.

SCRIPTURE REMINDS US

Psalm 56:3
"When I am afraid, I put my trust in You."

Romans 8:28
"And we know that in all things God works for the good of those who love Him, who have been called according to His purpose."

REFLECTIONS

What areas of my life are I allowing fear to overshadow my faith in God's promises?

How can I lean on past experiences of God's faithfulness to strengthen my trust in His timing today?

PRAYER

Heavenly Father,, thank You for always being with me and upholding me with Your righteous hand. Help me to trust You fully, even in moments of fear, uncertainty, or weakness. Refine me through challenges and shape me like a diamond so that my life may reflect Your glory. Strengthen my faith, calm my worries, and remind me that

Your timing is perfect. May I walk boldly, knowing that You are always by my side, preparing me for all that You have promised.

PERSONAL DEVOTIONAL WRITING

SECTION III:

BREAKTHROUGHS & MIRACLES

(Activation Faith)

THE 9 FRUIT OF THE HOLY SPIRIT

"But the Holy Spirit produces this kind of fruit in our lives: love, joy, peace, patience, kindness, goodness, faithfulness, gentleness, and self-control. There is no law against these things!" – Galatians 5:22-23

The nine fruits are the nine characteristics of God. When we are in an authentic and genuine relationship with God, His fruit becomes our fruit. We become a reflection of God in physical form. To bear these fruits, we must intentionally operate in four actions:

Action #1: Know Him

Knowing God goes beyond information; it requires relationship. The more we spend time with Him, through prayer, Scripture, and stillness, the more we understand His heart and His ways.

Action #2: Love Him

Loving God fuels obedience. When love leads, we don't follow God out of obligation but out of devotion, and our fruit becomes genuine rather than forced.

Action #3: Remember Him

Remembering God means keeping Him at the center of our daily lives, not just in moments of crisis. It is an awareness of His presence in every decision, conversation, and reaction.

Action #4: Imitate Him

Imitating God means aligning our behavior with His character. We choose patience when frustration would be easier. We choose kindness when offense feels justified. We choose self-control when impulse tries to rule.

These actions are the primary reason our fruit will grow and remain everlasting. We must constantly work every day to bear these fruits, as they are also the signs that reveal whether we are truly reflecting who God is. The more fruit we bear, the more we can teach and share the goodness of God with others.

If you are someone facing ongoing conflict at work or within your family. Without God, you may attempt to appear patient or kind while internally harboring resentment, anger, or pride. Over time, that strain shows. But when you remain connected to God, praying before responding, remembering who God is, and choosing to imitate His grace - your responses change. Peace replaces anxiety. Self-control replaces impulsive reactions. Faithfulness shows up in consistency. What others witness isn't effort or force. They simply witness Gods fruit harvesting in you.

SCRIPTURE REMINDS US:

John 15:4

"Remain in me, and I will remain in you. No branch can bear fruit by itself; it must remain in the vine."

There must be a clear understanding that these fruits cannot be harvested without God's help. Those who attempt to bear fruit without Him will experience continual disappointment. Those who falsely promote fruit they did not bear with God will eventually be exposed, regardless of the outcome.

Galatians 5:25

"Those who live by the Spirit should walk by the Spirit."

The only way to possess all nine fruits of the Spirit is to make God's vine your vine. Again, we must know Him, love Him, remember Him, and imitate Him every day of our lives.

REFLECTION

How will you execute the four actions moving forward?

What situations and relationships will we have to prune so that we can operate in our most authentic and genuine self to bear our fruit from the spirit?

PRAYER

Dear God, show me where I need to be to bear the fruits of the Spirit. Help me to prune properly and effectively. I know there have been times when I missed my season of harvest, but I come to You asking for help in every harvest season moving forward. Guide my steps in every way possible. Use my life as an example of an abundant life—one that is intentional in mind, body, and spirit.

Amen.

SURRENDER TO ISOLATION FOR EXPANSION

"But Jesus often withdrew to lonely places and prayed." - Luke 5:16

When God wants to expand you and position you for greater things, He may lead you into seasons of isolation. This separation is not punishment, it is preparation. In these moments, He stretches you beyond what you thought possible, removes distractions, and brings you into alignment with His will.

Isolation is God's way of coaching you in private. Like a best friend who corrects you in private before so that you don't make a fool of yourself in public, He prepares you to thrive when the time comes for your blessing to be revealed. This process may feel uncomfortable. You may feel vulnerable, disconnected, or even misunderstood at times but it is in these quiet, solitary spaces that God imparts wisdom, strategies, and clarity for your next season.

During this time, man-made rules and limitations may seem restrictive, but God's universal laws of purpose and alignment transcend them. He may lead you to break traditions or step outside comfort zones to position you for His glory. This is His way of showing you how to trust Him fully, even when the path is unseen or unconventional.

Consider the story of David before he became king. He spent years in the wilderness, isolated from his family and his kingdom, facing trials and hiding from enemies. Yet in that season, God was preparing him, teaching him humility, patience, and reliance on divine wisdom. When David stepped into the palace, he was ready. He had grown, matured, and had received strategies and insight that only those quiet seasons could provide. God will use every moment of isolation for your greater good. He wants to expand your mind, elevate your spirit, and increase your energy and capacity. Your time alone with Him is not wasted, it is a divine appointment for your growth, vision, and ultimate purpose. Embrace it. Listen closely. Receive instructions. And when the time comes, you will step out stronger, wiser, and fully prepared for what He has for you.

SCRIPTURE REMINDS US

Exodus 33:14

"The Lord replied, 'My Presence will go with you, and I will give you rest.'"

Even in isolation, God's presence accompanies you and equips you for the next level.

Isaiah 54:2

"Enlarge the place of your tent, stretch your tent curtains wide, do not hold back; lengthen your cords, strengthen your stakes."

Isolation is the preparation period for expansion—God stretches and strengthens you to contain more of His purpose.

REFLECTIONS

What areas of your life might God be asking you to embrace isolation in order to grow and prepare for your next season?

How can you shift your perspective to see seasons of solitude as a divine opportunity rather than a setback?

PRAYER

Heavenly Father, thank You for the seasons of solitude and preparation. Help me to surrender fully to Your timing and Your process. Teach me to embrace the isolation You place me in, knowing that You are stretching me, guiding me, and preparing me for greater expansion.

Guard my heart against fear, impatience, or doubt during this season. Open my ears to hear Your wisdom, my eyes to see Your plans, and my spirit to align fully with Your purpose. Let this time of preparation elevate my energy, my spirit, and my capacity so that I may step into the next season ready, strong, and fully aligned with You. Amen.

PERSONAL DEVOTIONAL WRITING

MIRACLES BEGIN WITH BELIEF

"I ask you again, does God give you the Holy Spirit and work miracles among you because you obey the law? Of course not! It is because you believe the message you heard about Christ. In the same way, "Abraham believed in God, and God counted him as righteous because of his faith." The real children of Abraham, then, are those who put their faith in God." - Galatians 3:5-7

The Holy Spirit and the manifestation of miracles become active in our lives when we truly believe in what God accomplished through Jesus Christ. Belief is not passive agreement. It is trust. It is alignment. It is living as if what God said is already true.

People who believe move differently. They pray differently. They endure differently. They expect differently. And because they expect differently, they act differently.

To believe means to accept something as true. Tto feel certain of its truth. It is having confidence in what exists, even when you do not yet see it. Belief does not require absolute proof; it requires trust in the One who cannot fail.

What God did through Jesus was not a one-time display of power meant to stay in history. It was a demonstration of what is possible when heaven and humanity are aligned. The same Spirit that empowered Jesus is available to us. What God did in Jesus, He can also do in you. Not so that you become worshipped, but so that God is revealed through you.

Miracles astonish us because they interrupt what we believe is possible. They disrupt limitation. They override logic. They remind us that what seems impossible to man is not impossible to God.

The deeper truth is that miracles are not always dramatic spectacles. Sometimes they are quiet transformations.

A hardened heart softening.
A generational cycle breaking.
A person choosing forgiveness when bitterness would have been easier.
A door opening after years of rejection.

When we operate in the Holy Spirit, we do not manufacture miracles, we partner with God's power. Our obedience becomes the vessel. Our faith becomes the doorway. Our lives become evidence.

The believer becomes a living example of God's light not by striving to look powerful, but by trusting deeply enough to walk boldly.

Consider a woman who has battled anxiety for years. She prays, but nothing changes immediately. She could conclude that God is absent. Instead, she chooses to believe that God is present and working even when she cannot see it.

Because she believes, she begins to act in alignment with that truth. She speaks differently over her life. She seeks wise counsel. She refuses to agree with fear. Slowly, strength replaces panic. Peace replaces dread. Her mind is renewed.

The miracle was not thunder from heaven. It was transformation from within.

And when others see her stability, her calm, her resilience, they ask, "*What changed?*" Her life becomes proof. That is how belief activates the Spirit. That is how miracles multiply. Not always in loudness and spotlight but in the surrender.

SCRIPTURE REMINDS US

Mark 9:23

"Jesus said unto him, If thou canst believe, all things are possible to him that believeth."

The condition was not perfection, status, or strength. Iit was belief. Jesus did not say all things are possible to the most talented or the most qualified. He said to the one who believes. Belief activates possibility. It shifts the atmosphere from limitation to expectation.

Romans 8:11

"But if the Spirit of him that raised up Jesus from the dead dwell in you, he that raised up Christ from the dead shall also quicken your mortal bodies by his Spirit that dwelleth in you."

The same Spirit that raised Jesus from the dead is not distant, it dwells in the believer. That means resurrection power is not just historical; it is personal. The Holy Spirit is not symbolic, it is always active.

REFLECTIONSS

In what area of my life am I waiting for proof before I choose to believe?

If I truly believed that the Holy Spirit was active within me, how would I think, speak, or act differently at this very moment?

PRAYER

Father God,

Thank You for the gift of belief. Thank You that faith is not something we manufacture, but something You awaken in us. Forgive us for the moments we have doubted Your power, Your timing, or Your presence in our lives.

Teach us to believe beyond what we see. Strengthen our confidence in who You are and in what You have already accomplished through Jesus Christ. Let us not live beneath the authority, power, and calling You have placed inside of us.

Holy Spirit, dwell in us fully. Remove fear, hesitation, and unbelief. Align our thoughts, our words, and our actions with heaven. Where there has been limitation, release possibility. Where there has been weakness, release strength. Where there has been delay, release divine movement.

Make our lives living evidence of Your power not for our glory, but so that others may see Your light through us. Help us to walk boldly, love deeply, forgive freely, and trust completely.

With unwavering belief in all that you do, Amen.

PERSONAL DEVOTIONAL WRITING

YOU ARE ALWAYS TAKEN CARE OF

"I am not saying this because I am in need, for I have learned to be content whatever the circumstances. I know what it is to be in need, and I know what it is to have plenty. I have learned the secret of being content in any and every situation, whether well fed or hungry, whether living in plenty or in want. I can do all this through him who gives me strength." - Philippians 4:11

We are always taken care of. God equips us with the strength to make the most of what we have, even when it feels like resources are scarce. Life may challenge us with struggles financial, relational, emotional, or otherwise but God never leaves us empty. His provision is constant, even when we cannot see it clearly.

Being "taken care of" doesn't always mean abundance in the world's terms. Sometimes it's the wisdom to make a difficult decision, the peace to endure a season of waiting, or the courage to use what little we have to accomplish His will. God reminds us that our cup is never completely empty; even in moments of lack, His presence fills us.

A modern example: Consider a young entrepreneur starting a business with limited funds and experience. On paper, it may look impossible, they might have just enough to cover a month of expenses and little else. Yet, through prayer, discernment, and faithful action, doors open: a mentor offers guidance, an unexpected client appears, or resources arrive just in time. The entrepreneur discovers that what they thought was "not enough" was actually exactly what God intended to begin the journey. God provides, often in ways that surpass our expectations.

Philippians 4:11 teaches contentment and learning to rely on God, even when circumstances seem limited. When we trust in Him, we realize that what we have now is sufficient. Our faith allows us to live in peace, knowing that God's provision is ongoing. Our "tank" is never on E because we serve an abundant God.

SCRIPTURE REMINDS US

Philippians 4:19

"And my God will meet all your needs according to the riches of His glory in Christ Jesus."

God's provision is constant and abundant, not limited by our perception or resources.

Psalm 23:1

"The Lord is my shepherd; I shall not want."

Even in times of apparent lack, God provides exactly ∞what we need to thrive and endure.

REFLECTION

Are there areas in your life where you feel "empty" or lacking, and how can you trust God to fill those spaces?

How can you use the resources and strengths you already have to fulfill God's purpose in your life today?

PRAYER

Heavenly Father, thank you for always taking care of me. Even when my resources feel limited, remind me that You are my provider and my strength. Help me to trust in Your abundance, even when I cannot see the full picture. Teach me to be content with what I have now and to use it wisely to fulfill Your purpose. Fill my heart, mind, and life with Your provision, and let me see that my cup is never empty because You are always faithful. Amen.

OCCUPY FORBIDDEN TERRITORIES

"For I know the plans I have for you," declares the Lord, "plans to prosper you and not to harm you, plans to give you hope and a future."
- Jeremiah 29:11

God has called us to occupy forbidden territories, spaces, opportunities, and positions that others never imagined we could reach. These are places where our presence will testify not to our own strength, but to the power, faithfulness, and glory of God. Forbidden territories are the areas where growth, breakthrough, and divine favor reside.

I heard about forbidden territories after watching a sermon by Sarah Jakes Roberts on YouTube. She describes these forbidden territories as:

- Places people never believed you would be
- Spaces others thought you could never afford
- Moving in ways uncommon in your industry
- Doing things that have never been done before
- Raising standards because of your elevated purpose and vision

Occupying these territories is not just about success, it's about obedience, faith, and demonstrating the power of God in your life. When you enter these spaces, do so fully aware that you represent God's glory. Illuminate the room with your presence, walk in confidence, and speak with authority. Let your actions and words reflect that God is with you and that His favor surrounds you. Forbidden territories are also about courage. They require stepping beyond comfort zones, ignoring limiting voices, and trusting God's assignment.

When you occupy spaces where you were once doubted or overlooked, you not only expand your own horizon, but you inspire others to pursue their God-given destiny. Your life becomes a living example that God equips those He calls for greatness.

Consider the story of Joseph in the Bible. From being sold into slavery to rising in Potiphar's house and eventually leading Egypt, Joseph occupied territories others would have deemed impossible for him. Every step he took in those "forbidden" spaces glorified God and positioned him for the destiny he was meant to fulfill.

God calls us to do the same: move boldly, act with purpose, and occupy spaces you were created for even if the world never expected you to.

SCRIPTURE REMINDS US

Matthew 5:14-16

"You are the light of the world. A town built on a hill cannot be hidden. Neither do people light a lamp and put it under a bowl. Instead they put it on its stand, and it gives light to everyone in the house. In the same way, let your light shine before others, that they may see your good deeds and glorify your Father in heaven."

Occupying forbidden territories is about letting God's light shine through you, leaving a lasting impact.

Ephesians 3:20-21

"Now to him who is able to do immeasurably more than all we ask or imagine, according to his power that is at work within us, to him be glory in the church and in Christ Jesus throughout all generations, for ever and ever! Amen."

God equips you with power beyond human expectation to occupy the spaces He has called you to.

REFLECTION

What "forbidden territories" is God calling you to step into, where others never expected you to be?

How can you bring God's light, authority, and presence into the spaces you currently occupy so that your impact is lasting?

PRAYER

Heavenly Father, thank you for calling me to occupy spaces that others never expected I would reach. Help me to move boldly, act with courage, and carry Your light into every room, situation, and opportunity. Remove doubt, fear, and hesitation from my heart. Teach me to operate with authority, integrity, and purpose so that every forbidden territory I enter reflects Your glory. Let my presence be a testimony of Your power, provision, and faithfulness. Guide me to the next space You have prepared and equip me to leave a lasting impact wherever I go. Amen.

WHAT YOU RELEASE DETERMINES WHAT YOU RECEIVE

"Pay careful attention to your own work, for then you will get the satisfaction of a job well done, and you won't need to compare yourself to anyone else. For we are each responsible for our own conduct." – Galatians 6:4-5

It is best to focus on what you are doing and not on the activities of others. When you don't, you're not giving 100% of yourself to achieve the best results. When we pay attention to our own lives, studying our own paths, walks, and actions—we can refine and perfect them. There is no need to compare ourselves to others, because they may be trying to be like you or may not truly be in alignment with themselves. God doesn't compare, and if you are His reflection, neither should you. Operate in your highest self. Reach your supreme being, and let your work and walk reflect your excellence.

When we take our eyes off our ordained work, which is our personal ministry, we are essentially telling God that what He placed within us isn't enough. That the gifts you have aren't enough. That the vision placed in you isn't fulfilling enough. That the blessings received after each faithful step weren't purposeful enough. That is deeply disrespectful. Why compare what others are releasing on their ordained path to yours? Even if you mimic what they have done, you will not receive the same results. You must focus on your own work and be content operating in excellence with what God has given you. We are responsible for what God has entrusted to us - our vision, our gifts and talents, and the support He places around us so that He alone receives the glory. Focus on every step. Turn good moves into great moves. Study long. Study hard. Simplify your strategies. Make your vision and message so clear that even a third grader can explain what you do, how you do it, and be excited about what you achieve after fulfilling the vision. We should always release at the highest capacity of the season we are in. What we release attracts new support, new blessings, and new visions. It reveals hidden gifts God has placed within us. What we receive cannot be measured, weighed, or compared when we are fully focused on our own work and experience the satisfaction of a job well done.

When you focus on what God has ordained and assigned *you*, something powerful happens - clarity sharpens, confidence grows, and results multiply. But you must remember that distractions is subtle. They often disguise themselves as curiosity, comparison, or "just checking in." But the moment your eyes drift from your lane, your energy begins to leak and drain. Excellence requires great attention, and attention requires great discipline.

Consider the story of Peter and Jesus walking on water. Peter was doing the impossible by walking toward Jesus until he noticed the wind and waves around him. The moment his focus shifted from Christ to the environment, he began to sink (read Matthew 14:28–31). The assignment didn't change. The conditions didn't change. Peter's *focus* did.

The same applies to our work, calling, and personal ministry. When God gives you an assignment, He equips you for *that* assignment, not for someone else's. Watching others too closely can make you abandon a strategy that was working, rush a season meant for refinement, or undervalue gifts that are still unfolding. Comparison will steal joy and interrupts obedience.

SCRIPTURE REMINDS US

Proverbs 4:25–26

"Let your eyes look directly forward, and your gaze be straight before you. Ponder the path of your feet; then all your ways will be sure."

God never asked you to manage someone else's calling. He asked you to steward *yours*. When you stay faithful to what's currently in your hands, you position yourself for what's coming next.

Faithfulness attracts increase and focus attracts momentum.

And the quiet truth is that when you do your work well, it speaks for you. There is no announcement required and no comparison needed.

Hebrews 12:1–2

"Let us run with endurance the race God has set before us. We do this by keeping our eyes on Jesus."

Your race is tailormade. Your pace is intentional. Your season is precise. So stay in it!

REFLECTIONS

Where has comparison distracted me from fully committing to the work God placed in my hands for this season?

What would change in my results, peace, or confidence if I gave my full attention to my own assignment instead of focusing on and comparing others?

PRAYER

Lord God, I ask for Your forgiveness for the times I did not fully value the gifts, talents, and visions You bestowed upon me in the past. Please forgive me, and grant me the grace to show up fully and boldly in the spaces You have prepared for me to do my greatest work. Allow my territory to stretch wide and my cup to overflow as I place my complete focus into the work You have assigned me.

May my work be acceptable in Your sight, and may it be used as You see fit to reveal Your glory and draw others closer to You. May my personal ministry flourish as a result of my godly focus and faithful obedience. I ask that You sustain my endurance and sharpen my vision, keeping my eyes clear and fixed on doing my best work on the canvas You have ordained for me. Amen.

STOP REACHING OUT & START REACHING UP

"Draw near to God, and He will draw near to you." - James 4:8

When we lack faith and confidence in ourselves, we typically reach out to others for a second opinion. We often hold their opinions in higher regard than our own. We constantly reach out when we're scared, going through life transitions, or facing hard lessons. Yet, we should be reaching up to God first—always.

When we do this first, we demonstrate strength in our confidence in God. We believe in ourselves and, more often than not, do just fine.

When we're operating from a place of trauma, we ask everyone for suggestions and make decisions that aren't based on truth, facts, or real information. But when we operate from a healed and healthy place, we look to God for help and answers. Therefore, we choose to reach up rather than reaching out to those who may love us but don't have the answers that only God can give.

Imagine you're facing a major life decision such as leaving a job, ending a relationship, starting a business, or moving to a new city. When fear is in the driver's seat, you call everyone you know. One person says, "Play it safe." Another says, "Take the risk." Someone else projects their own failures or fears onto your situation. Suddenly, you're overwhelmed and second-guessing everything.

But when you reach up first, you take the decision to God in prayer. You ask Him for wisdom, peace, and clarity. You sit with Him long enough to get a sense of direction. It's not just a feeling, but a knowing. Then, when you do seek counsel, you're not looking for permission or validation; you're seeking confirmation. The difference is powerful. God's voice steadies you, and external opinions no longer derail you.

SCRIPTURE REMINDS US:

Proverbs 3:5–6

"Trust in the Lord with all your heart and lean not on your own understanding; in all your ways submit to Him, and He will make your paths straight."

Psalm 46:10

"Be still, and know that I am God."

Stillness is often where clarity is born, nurtured, developed, and explored. When we reach up first, we give God space to lead instead of rushing to fill the silence with human opinions and limited knowing. People may love us deeply, but they don't have divine foresight. God does.

God is Genius because He always makes time and space for us to reach out, even when we *feel* like we don't have any. When we think there is no way, He always makes a way. When we believe there is no time, He creates moments for us to be still, teaching us how to use our time more effectively with Him involved. And when we think there is no room for change or for new things to be added to our lives for the better, He gently removes or shifts something, often without our awareness, so there is more than enough room for the answers to our prayers to arrive.

So let this be the moment of shift and change for you. Reach up before you reach out. Pray before you post. Listen before you react. Invite God into the decision before inviting the crowd. When God leads, confusion fades, peace follows, and alignment becomes undeniable.

Each day, set aside time to lift your spiritual arms through prayer and devotion. The more you do this, the clearer, easier, and more effectively you will hear God, and the higher your life will rise in alignment with His voice.

REFLECTION

In this season of your life, where are you being invited to trust God more than your own understanding or the opinions of others?

What does reaching up to God daily look like for you realistically and what needs to change for that to happen consistently?

PRAYER

God, I come to You to dwell in the space where You are. I surrender my time back to You. Show me where I need to go and who I need to become for the vision You blessed me to see from within. Shift what needs to be shifted so that I may live and breathe more abundantly. Help me maximize the time You have given me, so that not one second is wasted.

God, I reach up to You so You can help strengthen my faith muscles. In this season, I promise to reach up to You for the rest of my life, so that I may be an example of what happens when someone places their entire faith in You.

Amen.

PERSONAL DEVOTIONAL WRITING

BREAKTHROUGH OFTEN LOOKS LIKE BREAKDOWN

"Not only so, but we also glory in our sufferings, because we know that suffering produces perseverance; perseverance, character; and character, hope." - Romans 5:3-4

Sometimes, God's greatest blessings come disguised as our most difficult seasons. What looks like a breakdown such as loss, disappointment, or pressure, it is often the doorway to breakthrough. God uses trials, stretching, and challenging circumstances to prepare us for something bigger than we can imagine.

Consider Esther who was orphaned, living in exile, and initially an unknown member of the king's court. On the surface, her life seemed ordinary, even powerless. Yet, through a season of waiting, preparation, and alignment with God's plan, she was positioned to save the Jewish people from destruction. Her apparent "breakdown" being powerless in a foreign palace was the space God used to cultivate courage, wisdom, and influence. Her breakthrough came when she embraced her calling and acted boldly at the right time.

Imagine an entrepreneur who loses a business, faces financial hardship, and questions their own ability. From the outside, it appears like failure. Yet, through the struggle, they gain invaluable experience, refine their strategy, and build resilience. Later, they launch a new business that surpasses the original in impact and success. What initially seemed like a breakdown was actually the foundation for breakthrough.

Breakdowns test our faith, patience, and trust in God's timing. They challenge us to let go of control and rely fully on His power. Romans 5:3-4 reminds us that perseverance and character develop in these moments, producing hope and preparing us for what's next.

When you feel overwhelmed, remember that a breakdown does not mean the end. It signals that God is at work behind the scenes, stretching you, refining you, and positioning you for the next level. Trust Him, stay faithful, and remain aligned with His Word. Your breakthrough is often just on the other side of difficulty.

SCRIPTURE REMINDS US

Isaiah 61:3

"To grant to those who mourn in Zion—to give them a beautiful headdress instead of ashes, the oil of joy instead of mourning, and a garment of praise instead of a spirit of despair—so that they will be called oaks of righteousness, the planting of the Lord, that He may be glorified."

God transforms seasons of mourning and difficulty into joy, growth, and divine purpose.

2 Corinthians 12:9

"My grace is sufficient for you, for my power is made perfect in weakness."

This scripture reminds us that God's greatest power is often revealed when we feel weakest. What looks like a breakdown can actually be the stage where God demonstrates His strength.

REFLECTION

When facing a difficult season, how might God be using what feels like a breakdown to prepare you for a greater breakthrough?

What is one area of your life where you need to trust God's process instead of focusing on what appears to be falling apart?

PRAYER

Heavenly Father, thank you for reminding me that even in moments of pressure, confusion, or weakness, You are still working for my good. Help me to trust You when circumstances look like they are breaking down around me. Strengthen my faith so that I can see beyond the struggle and recognize the breakthrough You are preparing. Give me courage, patience, and wisdom to walk through every season with confidence in Your plan. Amen.

PERSONAL DEVOTIONAL WRITING

SECTION IV:

TRANSFORMATION & PURPOSE

(Living It Out)

EXTRAORDINARY LIGHTS CAN'T DWELL IN FAMILIAR LANDS

"Jesus left there and went to his hometown, accompanied by his disciples. When the Sabbath came, he began to teach in the synagogue, and many who heard him were amazed.

"Where did this man get these things?" they asked. "What's this wisdom that has been given him? What are these remarkable miracles he is performing? Isn't this the carpenter? Isn't this Mary's son and the brother of James, Joseph, Judas and Simon? Aren't his sisters here with us?" And they took offense at him.

Jesus said to them, "A prophet is not without honor except in his own town, among his relatives and in his own home." He could not do any miracles there, except lay his hands on a few sick people and heal them."
- Mark 6:1-5

Scripture teaches us and reminds us that our light does not always shine brightest in familiar lands or among familiar people, especially family and friends. Because of how they knew us in our upbringing and shared spaces of the past, they often assume we are the same and can't be no different than them. The unspoken narrative becomes: "*We all come from the same place,*" or "*We've seen you make mistakes*" or "*If it wasn't for me you wouldn't be who you are.*"

It can be frustrating, disappointing, and even heartbreaking when those who know us personally don't believe in our gifts or talents or fail to recognize that we may be chosen to lead at the highest level. But we must remind ourselves that even Jesus was not celebrated in His hometown the way He was in foreign lands.

Along my journey, I learned the importance of dwelling where you are loved and appreciated. In places where you are not, it becomes very difficult, sometimes nearly impossible to shine your light the way you were created to. Jesus was only able to perform a minimal number of miracles in His hometown because the people there did not believe in the light God had placed within Him. They questioned Him from the moment He arrived, even while witnessing the few miracles He performed: *"It can't be Him. Really? Jesus? Nah...what can He do? He's just a carpenter."*

I say to you - do not be disheartened or filled with sorrow. Instead, focus on the lands and the people who yearn for your light, your gifts, your message, and your miracles. Do God's work regardless of whether others believe in you or not. God will always position you in the right places to turn specific non-believers into believers.

We are not called to argue, debate, or spend sacred time trying to prove who we are. Let God handle that. Your responsibility is to show up consistently and shine. Do the work. Perform the miracles. Be one of God's blueprints and He will handle the rest.

SCRIPTURE REMINDS US

Mark 6:4

"A prophet is not without honor except in his own country, among his own relatives, and in his own house."

This scripture reminds us and reinforces the reality that rejection in familiar places is not a sign of failure, but often a sign of calling.

Matthew 5:14

"You are the light of the world. A city that is set on a hill cannot be hidden."

This reminds us that no amount of doubt from others can extinguish the light God has placed within us, especially when we continue to show up operating in it faithfully.

REFLECTIONS

In what spaces within your life are you trying to prove your light to people who are unwilling or unable to see it?

What would change if you redirected your energy toward the places and people who are prepared to receive what God has placed within you?

PRAYER

God, I thank You for the light You have placed within me. A light that does not depend on familiarity, approval, or validation from others. Help me release the need to be understood by those who are unable to see what You have called forth in me. Guard my heart from discouragement when my gifts are questioned, minimized, or overlooked.

Teach me to dwell where I am received, nurtured, and empowered to grow. Lead me to the people and places prepared for my assignment. Give me the wisdom to stop striving for acceptance and the courage to simply obey. Where rejection once caused hesitation, let my obedience produce extraordinary momentum.

Strengthen me to shine consistently, speak boldly, and move faithfully, whether I am celebrated or challenged. Use my life as a testimony that Your calling does not require consensus, only commitment. I trust You to handle the doubters while I focus on the work You've placed in my hands.

I surrender my need to prove and choose instead to produce. Let my fruit speak louder than my defense. I will show up, shine brightly, and do the work, knowing You will handle the rest.

Amen.

PERSONAL DEVOTIONAL WRITING

NEW WINE CAN'T BE ASSOCIATED WITH OLD SKIN

"Besides, who would patch old clothing with new cloth? For the new patch would shrink and rip away from the old cloth, leaving an even bigger tear than before and no one puts new wine into old wineskins. For the wine and the skins would both be lost. New wine calls for new wineskins." – Mark 2:21-22

We can't speak of what was and use to be. We can't operate with the same system and language. There must be a new narrative that is now being played and talked about. A consistency which is the new wine skin. The things that hold the new you in place. To never, for one moment, give you the space to believe that who you use to be is better than who you transformed into. It is a must to always keep new wine connected and in new wine skin. Show off who God turned you into with no timidness. Renewed!

We can't move forward while carrying old habits, unresolved issues, trauma, and emotional baggage. When we go through a transformation, we must be made new, unrecognizable to the circles and environments we once dwelled in. We must establish new ways, habits, and disciplines to ensure we never return to the old patterns.

When we pass through the wilderness, we are stripped completely and rebuilt with new vision, methods, strength, insight, wisdom, and a higher frequency and energy.

We can't continue speaking about what was and what used to be. We can't operate with the same systems or language. There must be a new narrative. One that is now being lived and spoken. This consistency becomes the new wineskin: the structure that holds the new you in place. It leaves no room, even for a moment, to believe that who you once were is better than who you have become.

It is essential to keep new wine connected to new wineskins. Show the world who God has transformed you into without timidity, without apology. Renewed.

Think of the Israelites after leaving Egypt. Physically, they were free, but mentally, they were still enslaved. They longed for familiar systems, even when those systems oppressed them. God had to recondition their thinking before they could enter the Promised Land. The old mindset could not sustain the new territory (Exodus 16; Numbers 14). Had God brought them into abundance without transformation, they would have destroyed what they were given.

The same principle applies today. You cannot speak the language of deliverance while operating with the systems of bondage. You cannot steward new wine with old wineskins. A new narrative must replace the old one with new habits, new disciplines, new language, and new boundaries. These become the wineskin that protects the transformation.

Consistency is the container. Discipline is the guardrail. Without them, the old version will try to negotiate its way back in. That's why God insists on making renewal as a way of life.

SCRIPTURE REMINDS US

2 Corinthians 5:17

"Therefore, if anyone is in Christ, the new creation has come: The old has gone, the new is here!"

Romans 12:2

"Don't copy the behavior and Zcustoms of this world, but let God transform you into a new person by changing the way you think."

These scriptures affirm that transformation requires separation from former patterns and an intentional renewal of the mind.

REFLECTIONS

What old habits, mindsets, or emotional attachments am I still carrying that could damage what God is doing now?

What new disciplines or boundaries do I need to establish to protect the version of me God has already transformed?

PRAYER

Dear God, I thank you for where you placed me seen and unseen. I thank you for the shifts and elevations in my life. Thank you for the valleys and alleys I had to walk through that shaped me. Thank you for the grace you gave me in the past. But now, I am asking you to transform me into who you need me to be. Change my walk, talk, and appearance. Make me a new person starting right now. May I be unrecognizable in the familiar lands in which I dwell and used to dwell. Help me break old habits and establish new ones for the fulfillment of your purpose. May all those who lay eyes on me, in every room I walk into, see you dwelling within and around me. May my voice vibrate the ear drums of every person that hears me. May your power be my strength like no other. And may my surrendering to be made new be the complete ingredient to a new and fulfilling life. Amen.

THE HOLY SPIRIT HIBERNATES IN YOU

"Don't you realize that your body is the temple of the Holy Spirit, who lives in you and was given to you by God? You do not belong to yourself, for God bought you with a high price. So you must honor God with your body." – 1 Corinthians 6:19-20

The Holy Spirit lives within us and can be activated in our lives at any moment. When we live with this awareness, we begin to move through our day guided by the Spirit. Our decisions, thoughts, and actions can all be shaped by a Spirit-led mind.

Because the Holy Spirit dwells within us, we must also be mindful of what we put into our bodies and what we allow into our hearts and minds. Our bodies are temples of the Holy Spirit, and the way we live should reflect the presence of God within us.

Imagine what your temple would look like if you consciously allowed the Holy Spirit to guide you. What would you be saying? What would you be thinking? What kind of energy and influence would you attract when you are walking in the Spirit?

Fasting and prayer help detox the temple. They clear distractions, realign our hearts with God, and allow our lives to radiate His love and glory more clearly.

Each day, it should be our goal to live with the Holy Spirit actively leading us. When we do this, God begins to make crooked paths straight. Our presence can shift environments, and our lives become an example of God's glory that draws others closer and inspires them to want to know the God we serve.

Imagine someone walking into a workplace where tension and negativity fill the room. Instead of reacting with frustration like everyone else, that person chooses to pause, pray, and respond with patience, wisdom, and encouragement.

Their words calm the situation. Their attitude changes the atmosphere. Others begin to feel a sense of peace around them. That is what happens when someone is living with the Holy Spirit actively guiding them. Their temple is aligned with God, and His presence begins to influence not only their life but the environment around them.

When the Holy Spirit is active within us, we don't just change ourselves, we help change the atmosphere wherever we go.

SCRIPTURE REMINDS US

Galatians 5:16

"So I say, walk by the Spirit, and you will not gratify the desires of the flesh."

Romans 8:14

"For those who are led by the Spirit of God are the children of God."

REFLECTION

How can I practically allow the Holy Spirit to guide my thoughts, words, and actions today?

What habits or distractions might I need to remove to fully honor my body as a temple of the Holy Spirit?

PRAYER

God, Thank You for placing Your Spirit within me. Help me to remain aware of Your presence and to walk each day guided by Your Spirit.

Teach me to honor my body as a temple and to make choices that reflect Your glory. Detox my heart, mind, and body from anything that blocks Your Spirit. May my words, actions, and energy radiate Your love and draw others closer to You. Lead me, Holy Spirit, so that my life is a living example of Your power and grace. Amen.

APPOINTED AND ANOINTED

"You didn't choose me. I chose you. I appointed you to go and produce lasting fruit, so that the father will give you whatever you ask for, using my name." – John 15:16

God knew us before we even knew ourselves. Even as we grow and change into new versions of ourselves, He still knows every step of our journey to becoming who we are meant to be. When He chooses you, He makes you an example to the world of what happens when you stay connected and believe in Him. The fruits of obedience are everlasting, like His love. He never waivers, even if we do. And as long as we ask in His name, including for forgiveness, we will witness His wonders.

The life of John the Baptist is a blueprint for how to study, learn, prepare, lead, and live faithfully in a way that pleases God. John focused entirely on obedience. He dedicated his energy to one purpose: announcing the coming of Jesus. In the wilderness, John heard God's direction and instruction, and he prepared himself, stayed ready, and waited for the divine timing God had ordained.

Most people forget that John the Baptist had no position of power but spoke with incredible and irresistible power authority. He made it clear and direct to the people to not focus on him but the message he was ordained and tasked with to share with the masses. John the Baptist words moved people because he only spoke truth.

Most people forget that John had no political or social position, yet he spoke with incredible authority and influence. His words were clear, direct, and irresistible because he focused not on himself, but on the message God had entrusted to him. John's power came from his obedience, his faith, operating only in truth, and his unwavering commitment to the purpose God had given him.

Just like John, God gives each of us a purpose. We must remain dedicated to that purpose, especially through our wilderness moments and times of preparation. God does not promise an easy or comfortable life to those who serve Him, but He can transform our lives into living testimonies of His power and faithfulness—demonstrating what happens when we trust and follow Him completely.

SCRIPTURE REMINDS US

Luke 1:17

"And he will go on before the Lord, in the spirit and power of Elijah, to turn the hearts of the parents to their children and the disobedient to the wisdom of the righteous—to make ready a people prepared for the Lord."

John's life reminds us that preparation, obedience, and purpose precede God's timing.

John 3:30

"He must become greater; I must become less."

John's humility and focus on God's mission show us the power of prioritizing purpose over position or recognition.

REFLECTION

What wilderness moments or seasons of preparation in your life might God be using to ready you for your purpose?

Are there ways you are focusing on yourself rather than the mission God has given you, and how can you realign?

PRAYER

Heavenly Father, thank You for knowing me before I even knew myself. Help me stay connected to You and trust in Your timing. Like John the Baptist, give me the focus, obedience, and humility to walk in the purpose You have set before me. Keep me ready for every moment You prepare, and guide my words, actions, and heart so that they reflect Your truth. May my life be a testimony of Your power, faithfulness, and love, pointing others to You rather than myself.

BE A LIVING SANCTUARY

"Each one will be like a shelter from the wind and a refuge from the storm, like streams of water in the desert and the shadow of a great rock in a thirsty land."- Isaiah 32:2

A spiritual sanctuary is a sacred, protected space that is physical or internal. It provides an offering of refuge, peace, and connection to the divine or a deeper self, providing solace from worldly chaos and facilitating rest, reflection, and spiritual renewal through practices like prayer, meditation, or communion with nature. It can be a temple, a quiet corner in nature, a specific relationship, or even an internal state of being, representing ultimate belonging and safe.

Scripture reminds us that God desires His presence to dwell within us: *"Do you not know that you are God's temple and that God's Spirit dwells in you?"* - 1 Corinthians 3:16

When we live with this awareness, our daily decisions begin to matter even more. The way we invest our time, where we place our attention, and the choices we make each day reveal whether we are creating peace or chaos for the people around us.

Many of us walk through life without realizing that we are answered prayers for someone else. God often sends people into our lives to provide encouragement, comfort, wisdom, or simply a safe place to breathe.

But we cannot fulfill those prayers if we fill our lives with distractions, unhealthy habits, or environments that prevent us from being a place of peace for others.

Jesus Himself invited the weary into a place of spiritual rest when He said: *"Come to me, all you who are weary and burdened, and I will give you rest."* - *Matthew 11:28*

As followers of God, we are called to reflect that same spirit of refuge and compassion. There is a divine beauty and honor in being a sanctuary for others during difficult times. Whether someone holds great influence in leadership or struggles in the deepest trenches of poverty, everyone experiences moments when the weight of life feels overwhelming.

To be the person who helps guide someone back to peace is powerful.

Scripture reminds us that God uses us as vessels of comfort: *"Praise be to the God and Father of our Lord Jesus Christ... who comforts us in all our troubles, so that we can comfort those in any trouble with the comfort we ourselves receive from God."* - 2 Corinthians 1:3–4

When we allow God to cultivate peace within us, our relationships and conversations become extensions of our sanctuary. People feel safe to be honest, vulnerable, and authentic in our presence. Real connection begins to grow.

In those sacred moments of conversation, encouragement, and care, God moves among us.Where love, truth, and compassion exist, God is present. And the relationships we nurture become places where grace flows freely and healing quietly begins.

To live as a sanctuary is not about perfection. It is about creating space in your heart where God's presence is strong enough that others can encounter peace simply by being near you. And when you become that kind of person, God blesses your life in ways you could never fully imagine.

SCRIPTURE TEACHES US

Psalm 46:1

"God is our refuge and strength, an ever-present help in trouble."

This verse reminds us that God Himself is the ultimate sanctuary.

When we stay connected to Him, His peace and strength flow through us, allowing us to become a refuge for others who are facing difficult seasons.

Romans 12:13

"Share with the Lord's people who are in need. Practice hospitality."

Hospitality in Scripture is not only about opening your home - it is about opening your heart, presence, and spirit to others. When we practice compassion, listening, and kindness, we create a spiritual space where people feel welcomed, safe, and valued.

REFLECTION

What habits or distractions in my life might be preventing me from being a place of peace and refuge for others?

How can I intentionally cultivate God's presence in my daily life so that my relationships reflect His peace and compassion?

PRAYER

Heavenly Father,
Thank You for being my refuge and sanctuary. Fill my heart with Your peace so that others may experience comfort, safety, and hope through my presence. Help me to guard my time, my decisions, and my spirit so that I can reflect Your love in every relationship. Use my life as a place where Your presence dwells and where others can find rest. Expand my sanctuary in all that I do in each minute, hour, day, week, and year ahead. Amen.

PERSONAL DEVOTIONAL WRITING

SPRINKLE AND RESTORE

"I will sprinkle clean water on you, and you will be clean; I will cleanse you from all your impurities and from all your idols. I will give you a new heart and put a new spirit in you; I will remove from you your heart of stone and give you a heart of flesh. And I will put my Spirit in you and move you to follow my decrees and be careful to keep my laws"
- Ezekiel 36:25-27

God promises to make all things new, restoring both our physical and spiritual lives. He offers to wash away our sins, give us a new heart, and place His Spirit within us. While we cannot change the past, God provides a clean start in the present and a hopeful future.

Transformation is a process. It doesn't always happen instantly, but it is always intentional. God's restoration may begin in small ways: learning to forgive ourselves for mistakes, choosing to treat others differently, or finding the courage to pursue dreams we once thought impossible. For example, someone who failed in business or relationships may feel hopeless, but God can transform those experiences into wisdom, strength, and preparation for future success. He equips us with the power and resilience we need to fulfill His purpose.

No matter how many mistakes we've made or how far we've strayed, God gives a fresh start even when others would not. Consider the story of Peter, who denied Jesus three times yet was restored and became a foundational leader in the early church. God does not measure our worth by the errors of the past; He measures it by our willingness to surrender and step into His plan.

Transformation is not just about personal renewal; it is about stepping fully into the purpose God has for our lives. When we embrace His power and guidance, we become living examples of His love and faithfulness. God can take a broken heart, a failed business, a lost opportunity, or even years of regret, and turn it into a platform for growth, leadership, and influence.

Your past does not define your future. God's promise to transform and restore is bigger than any setback. He calls you to rise, to step into your purpose, and to live as a testimony of His faithfulness.

SCRIPTURE REMINDS US

2 Corinthians 5:17

"Therefore, if anyone is in Christ, the new creation has come: The old has gone, the new is here!"

God transforms us completely, giving us a fresh start and a new identity in Him.

Ezekiel 36:26

"I will give you a new heart and put a new spirit in you; I will remove from you your heart of stone and give you a heart of flesh."

God's restoration is both internal and spiritual, preparing us for the purpose He has for our lives.

REFLECTIONS

In what areas of your life do you need God's transformation to step fully into your purpose?

Are there past mistakes or regrets you are holding onto that God wants you to release so you can embrace His fresh start?

PRAYER

Heavenly Father, thank You for Your promise to make all things new.

Wash away my sins, renew my heart, and fill me with Your Spirit. Help me release the past and embrace the fresh start You provide today. Transform my mind, my spirit, and my actions so that I am fully equipped to walk in the purpose You have for my life. Let Your power guide me and Your promises sustain me, that I may reflect Your love, grace, and faithfulness in everything I do. Amen.

PERSONAL DEVOTIONAL WRITING

YOU ARE ROYAL BLOOD

"I say, "You are gods; you are all children of the Most High. But you will die like mere mortals and fall like every other ruler." – Psalms 82:67

There is something powerful about remembering who you are.

Scripture tells us that we are children of the Most High. That means we are not random, not forgotten, and not powerless. We are born of divine purpose. Royalty flows through our spiritual lineage not because of our own greatness, but because of the One we belong to.

Even with all this, Psalm 82 carries a warning. Though called "gods" (*a reference to those given authority*), we can still died like mere mortals when we forgot our responsibility and misused our position. It's a clear understanding that identity without obedience leads to downfall.

We are created in God's image (Genesis 1:27). We carry His imprint. His creativity. His authority to steward. His capacity to love, build, and lead. On this earth, we are entrusted with influence. But influence must remain aligned with our Father.

The enemy's strategy is subtle. It's distraction. It's fear. It's insecurity. It's stress. If he can keep us doubting who we are, we will never walk boldly in what we've been given. Royal blood doesn't beg. Royal blood doesn't shrink back. Royal blood stands firm in truth.

This doesn't mean we are equal to God. It means we are empowered by Him.

When you truly understand that you belong to the Most High, fear loses its grip. Stress no longer rules you. You begin to move with confidence. Not arrogance, but assurance. You realize that favor rests on obedience, and authority flows from alignment.

All creation responds to divine order. When you walk in alignment with the Creator, you carry His peace, His authority, and His presence into every room.

We cannot live as if we are unaware of our power or our purpose. To do so is to shrink back from the very authority God entrusted to us. We are called to be vessels and living representations of the all-powerful, all-knowing God. What a disservice it is to operate beneath the royal authority we have been anointed with as children of His royal bloodline.

Yet even as members of this royal family, we must remain humble and wise. Life is still fragile. We must learn to think twice and speak once. Listen more than we talk. Observe and meditate more than we react in impatience or hesitation. Though we carry divine purpose, we still live in mortal bodies. We can stumble. We can fall. We were perfectly created, yet placed in imperfect flesh to fulfill royal assignments in a world that often magnifies what it calls our flaws.

God does not make mistakes in how He formed us to reflect Him. Not one detail is accidental. We must trust His Word at all times and walk with our heads lifted even when circumstances seem low, when things appear to be dying around us, or when our personal world feels like it is collapsing. We are not exempt from our Father's teaching moments. Those seasons refine us so that we wear our crown with integrity.

In Proverbs 3:5–6, we are reminded: *"Trust in the Lord with all your heart; do not depend on your own understanding. Seek His will in all you do, and He will show you which path to take."* This centers us. No matter how strategic our plans may be, God's plan is wiser and more effective. Our knowledge, experience, and even our crowned posture do not remove our human limitation. In the end, we are still mortal and cannot see what God sees in full.

Blessings often arrive from unexpected places. Breakthroughs rarely announce themselves in advance. The most seasoned experts and consultants cannot predict where God will move on your behalf. So, work faithfully. Trust deeply. Even when your crown feels heavy, keep wearing it with honor.

Most of the time, you will not see how God is orchestrating the outcome. But when it unfolds, you will look back with gratitude.

. Remember who you are, a child of the Most High. Walk in every room with the quiet confidence of divine authority. Not arrogance, but assurance. The same God who moves mountains and parts seas is the One you reflect and represent.

SCRIPTURE REMINDS US

Romans 8:16–17

"The Spirit himself testifies with our spirit that we are God's children. Now if we are children, then we are heirs—heirs of God and co-heirs with Christ..."

This affirms our "royal bloodline". We are not just believers, we are heirs. Royalty isn't just hype; it's our divine inheritance. But inheritance also comes with maturity, responsibility, and alignment.

2 Corinthians 4:7

"But we have this treasure in jars of clay to show that this all-surpassing power is from God and not from us."

We carry divine authority, yet we live in mortal vessels. The power is real but it flows from God, not ego. We have a royal identity but a humble container.

REFLECTIONS

Am I walking in divine confidence, or am I shrinking back because of fear, distraction, or insecurity? Where in my life am I operating beneath the authority God has already given me?

When my "crown feels heavy," do I lean into trust and obedience, or do I try to control outcomes with my own limited understanding?

PRAYER

Father God,

Thank You for calling me Your child and placing royal purpose within me. Thank you for the anointing and always showing up when my crown seems to be slipping down. Help me to walk in the authority You've given me without pride, and in humility without shrinking back. When fear tries to distract me or when my crown feels heavy, remind me who I belong to. Teach me to trust You beyond what I see, to move with wisdom, and to represent You with integrity in every room I enter. Strengthen me in my mortal moments and align my heart with Your perfect will.

I receive Your grace, Your guidance, and Your favor today and always. Amen.

ALIGNMENT
CHANGES EVERYTHING

"Submit yourselves, then, to God. Resist the devil, and he will flee from you. Come near to God and he will come near to you." - James 4:7-8

Alignment with God changes everything. When our thoughts, actions, and priorities are in sync with His will, life begins to flow according to His design. Misalignment creates confusion, frustration, and missed opportunities, but obedience and submission open the door to clarity, favor, and supernatural provision.

Alignment is more than just following rules, it's a posture of the heart. It's deciding daily to prioritize God's kingdom over our own agendas, to seek His wisdom instead of leaning solely on our understanding, and to allow Him to direct every decision we make.

Consider a business owner who consistently seeks God's guidance in every deal, hires employees aligned with His values, and manages finances with integrity may face challenges but doors often open in ways they could never plan alone. Opportunities appear at the right time, partnerships form naturally, and the business grows sustainably. Alignment with God doesn't remove challenges, but it positions us to navigate them with divine favor and wisdom.

Even when life feels chaotic, alignment with God steadies the heart and mind. Psalm 37:23-24 reminds us that though we may stumble, God holds us steady. James 4:7-8 teaches that submission to God gives us authority over challenges and brings His presence closer to us. When we seek first His kingdom (Matthew 6:33), everything else begins to fall into place.

When our life is aligned with God, even ordinary moments carry extraordinary purpose. Decisions become clearer. Relationships become stronger. Opportunities become visible. Alignment doesn't just change circumstances; it changes the way we see and experience life itself.

SCRIPTURE REMINDS US

Proverbs 3:5-6

"Trust in the Lord with all your heart and lean not on your own understanding; in all your ways submit to him, and he will make your paths straight."

Psalm 37:23-24

"The Lord makes firm the steps of the one who delights in him; though he may stumble, he will not fall, for the Lord upholds him with his hand."

REFLECTION

In what areas of your life might you be out of alignment with God's will, and how can you correct it today?

How would your decisions, relationships, or opportunities change if you fully submitted your plans and priorities to God?

PRAYER

Heavenly Father, thank you for guiding my steps and for the promise that alignment with You changes everything. Help me to trust You completely, to submit every part of my life to Your will, and to seek Your kingdom first in all I do. Show me the areas where I am out of alignment and give me the courage and wisdom to adjust. Steady my heart, sharpen my vision, and open doors that only Your favor can provide. Let my life reflect Your purpose and may every decision I make bring glory to Your name. Amen.

SECTION V:
WALKING WITH GOD DAILY
(Sustained Faith)

PRESERVE AND PROTECT FOR EVERLASTING SAKE

"Watch out that you do not lose what we have worked so hard to achieve. Be diligent so that you receive your full reward." – 2 John 1:8

We must preserve and protect what we have worked hard to attain. Nothing should be taken for granted. Be intentional about safeguarding your family, maintaining your reputation, nurturing healthy relationships, preserving your peace, respecting the boundaries you've established, and protecting the things you have purchased or earned.

At the same time, focus on claiming everything you deserve. Don't leave blessings or opportunities on the table. When you put in the necessary work and meet the requirements, confidently ask for and expect your full reward. Work with brilliance, move with excellence, and give your best effort in all areas. This is the foundation of diligence which is a determined pursuit of all that God has prepared for you

Imagine an entrepreneur who spent years building a business from the ground up. They've invested time, energy, and resources, and now their company is thriving.

- **Preserve:** They make sure contracts are secure, finances are protected, and their team is treated well to maintain loyalty.
- **Pursue:** They continue innovating, investing in growth, and seeking opportunities to expand revenue and impact.

By protecting what they've earned and actively pursuing new rewards, they maximize the fruits of their labor. This is high level diligence that doesn't just keep blessings but multiplies them.

SCRIPTURE REMINDS US

Proverbs 10:4

"Lazy hands make for poverty, but diligent hands bring wealth."

Galatians 6:9

"Let us not become weary in doing good, for at the proper time we will reap a harvest if we do not give up."

REFLECTIONS

What areas of your life require more diligence to preserve what you've worked hard to achieve?

Are there blessings or opportunities you have left unclaimed, and how can you actively pursue them today?

PRAYER

Heavenly Father, thank You for the work You have allowed me to accomplish. Help me to protect and preserve all that I have earned and all that I have been entrusted with. Give me diligence, focus, and wisdom to pursue every blessing You have promised. May I work with excellence, safeguard my relationships, and steward my resources well. Teach me not to leave anything on the table but to claim the full reward You have prepared for me. Let my life reflect diligence, faith, and Your glory. Amen.

PERSONAL DEVOTIONAL WRITING

LEAD
WITH STRENGTH AND CLARITY

"Be strong and courageous, for you are the one who will lead these people to possess all the land I swore to their ancestors I would give to them." – Joshua 1:6

The scripture, along with the entire first chapter of the Book of Joshua, emphasizes the importance of being strong and courageous. This instruction is repeated multiple times so that it fully sinks in. It reveals a spiritual key to breakthroughs and to becoming a master of your faith.

Joshua was given the blessing and the responsibility to lead a nation. He was chosen to lead a generation into the Promised Land that the previous generation could not enter because of their lack of faith, strength, and courage. Many of them failed to follow God's instructions and neglected spending devoted time with Him.

Joshua, however, led with strength and conviction. The people who followed him trusted him and promised to obey his leadership because they saw his courage and faith in God. Joshua carried authority and did not hesitate to give instructions as God directed him. His confidence did not come from himself, it came from his relationship with God.

In the same way, we are called to move with strength and courage so that we can expand the work God has placed in our hands. Nothing truly grows without clarity and unity. There must be clarity in the vision and in the instructions that God places within you. There must also be strength in your faith, steadiness in your actions, and protection over the momentum that God is building.

When these things align, clarity, faith, courage, and unity movement begins to happen with grace. Progress becomes visible to everyone around you. However, it is also important to maintain spiritual protection and covering so that nothing interferes with what God is building.

This is why daily devotion with God is essential. Spending time with Him provides direction, strength, and the courage needed to lead and move forward.

A modern example of this principle can be seen in someone who is called to launch a business, ministry, or organization that serves others. Often, the vision God gives may be larger than what others around them initially understand. Some people may doubt the direction, while others may hesitate to follow.

However, when a leader remains committed to prayer, devotion, and obedience to God's guidance, clarity begins to form. With courage, they continue moving forward even when challenges arise. Over time, others begin to see the vision clearly and join in the mission. What once seemed uncertain begins to grow, expand, and impact lives.

Just like Joshua, leadership requires faith, courage, and a daily connection with God. When those qualities are present, the path toward the promise
becomes clear.

SCRIPTURE REMINDS US

Joshua 1:9

"Have I not commanded you? Be strong and courageous. Do not be afraid; do not be discouraged, for the Lord your God will be with you wherever you go."

Isaiah 41:10

"So do not fear, for I am with you; do not be dismayed, for I am your God. I will strengthen you and help you; I will uphold you with my righteous right hand."

REFLECTIONS

In what area of your life is God calling you to step forward with greater strength and courage right now?

Are you consistently spending time with God so that your leadership, decisions, and actions are guided by His direction rather than fear or uncertainty?

PRAYER

Heavenly Father, thank You for calling us to walk in strength and courage. Help us to trust Your guidance and remain faithful to the vision and purpose You have placed in our lives. Give us clarity in our decisions, steadiness in our faith, and the courage to lead where You have called us to lead. Protect the work You are building through us and keep our hearts disciplined in daily devotion with You. May everything we do bring glory to Your name. Amen.

PRAYER IS PARTNERSHIP

"In fact, for days I mourned, fasted, and prayed to God of heaven." - Nehemiah 1:4

We must pour our hearts out to God. We must share everything we feel with Him, whatever hurts us and whatever brings us joy. We are called to pour it all out before God. Prayer is one of the most powerful and effective ways to communicate with the God who dwells within us. Prayer brings our life partner, which is God, to the forefront so we can discuss the plan for the season we are in and confront what lies ahead.

When we lack prayer time, we lack communication in the greatest relationship of our lives, which is our relationship with God. Show me your spiritual relationship and communication patterns with God, and I can tell you a great deal about your relationships and communication patterns with people in the physical world.

Nehemiah's life is a powerful example of prayer and work in action. His focus was always on improving his situation while remaining pleasing in God's sight. We can learn much from Nehemiah's prayer walk. His prayers were effective because they centered on five key areas:

- Praise
- Thanksgiving
- Commitment
- Clear and Specific Request
- Repentance

These five areas allow us to be in full and honest communication with

God. Through prayer, we are able to:

- Clarify vision when things feel unclear
- Gain understanding about the problems we face
- Fulfill the ordained tasks God has given us to complete
- Receive God's power to overturn and shift circumstances in our favor
- Bring order to situations that are currently out of order

Nehemiah maximized and leveraged all his resources - his experience, knowledge, and organizational skills, while remaining rooted in prayer to complete the work God had assigned him. He prayed for success and for favor with the king. What remains true now, as it was then, is the importance of clarity. Clarity in life produces confidence, and confidence makes you a more effective and sought-after leader.

Nehemiah modeled what it means to live a life committed to God-honoring leadership. To thrive and grow beyond our own imagination, we must remain committed to honoring God's leadership in our lives through the way we pray and communicate with Him. Everything we do in our leadership role over our own lives should be done in recognition of God. This requires clarity...clarity of vision and clarity of need because when we encounter those who can assist us, we must be clear, confident, and intentional in our ask.

SCRIPTURE REMINDS US

Philippians 4:6

"Do not be anxious about anything, but in every situation, by prayer and petition, with thanksgiving, present your requests to God."

This scripture reinforces the idea of full communication with God bringing everything to Him, not selectively, and trusting Him with both the burden and the outcome.

Psalm 145:18

"The Lord is near to all who call on Him, to all who call on Him in truth."

This verse affirms that honest, heartfelt prayer draws us into closer alignment with God. When we pour out our hearts in truth, God meets us with presence, clarity, and direction.

REFLECTION

What areas of your life are you carrying silently that God is inviting you to bring to Him openly in prayer?

How might your leadership, decisions, and relationships change if prayer became your first response instead of your last choice?

PRAYER

Dear God, help me strengthen my communication with You so that I may walk in clarity in all things. I come before You with humility, fully aware that I cannot walk this journey without You. Teach me to bring every burden, every question, and every decision to You in prayer, instead of carrying them in silence.

Allow me to see through Your eyes, hear with Your ears, speak with Your wisdom, and walk in Your footsteps. Align my heart with Your will so that my leadership, choices, and relationships reflect Your truth. Give me the courage to move mountains of fear and doubt, and the faith to part the Red Seas that stand in my way.

As I grow in communication with You, help me lead my life with confidence, peace, and purpose. May my prayers be clear, my faith be active, and my obedience be complete. I surrender every area of my life to You, trusting that where You lead, provision, clarity, and victory will follow.

Amen.

YOUR PROMISE LAND

"I promised you what I promised Moses. Wherever you set foot, you will be on land I have given you." – Joshua 1:3

We must follow God's lead if we want to succeed at the highest level. God never breaks His promises. When we align ourselves with His will, He gives us more than we could ever imagine.

Every step we take in this lifetime is already known and prepared by God. When we truly understand this, we begin to realize that both the fruitful land and the desolate land belong to us. Each place we step into carries purpose.

Wherever we go, we must walk with authority, knowing that every step is part of our journey. Even when the land appears difficult, uncertain, or uncomfortable, it still has meaning. Our human emotions may try to define the season we are in, but our spiritual vision must lead us instead.

We must learn to view the land before us with spiritual eyes rather than emotional reactions. God has assigned each step, each place, and each experience for our growth.

Trust the land God has given you.
Trust the experiences you cultivate in the land He has placed before you.
It is part of your calling, your journey, and your story.

Think of a farmer who receives a large piece of land. Part of it is fertile and ready for crops, while another section is rocky and difficult to work. At first, the farmer might only see the productive fields as valuable. However, over time he realizes that the rocky ground contains minerals that strengthen the soil and help the harvest grow stronger.

In the same way, God gives us seasons that feel fruitful and seasons that feel difficult. The successful moments and the challenging ones are both part of the territory God has given us. When we trust His promise and continue stepping forward in faith, every part of the land eventually reveals its purpose.

So, don't judge the land too quickly because God sees the full harvest long before we see the first seed.

SCRIPTURE REMINDS US:

Proverbs 3:5–6

"Trust in the Lord with all your heart and lean not on your own understanding; in all your ways submit to Him, and He will make your paths straight."

Romans 8:28

"And we know that in all things God works for the good of those who love Him, who have been called according to His purpose."

REFLECTIONS

What "land" or season has God currently placed you in that you may be resisting or questioning?

How might God be preparing you through the difficult places you are walking through right now?

PRAYER

Heavenly Father, Thank You for ordering my steps and preparing the path before me. Help me to trust the land You have given me, whether it feels fruitful or difficult. Give me spiritual vision so that I do not judge my journey through emotion but through faith. Teach me to walk with confidence, knowing that every step has purpose and meaning in Your plan. Strengthen my heart to trust Your promises and to move forward with courage. Amen.

KEEP GOING
ANYWAY

"Trust in the Lord with all your heart and lean not on your own understanding; in all your ways submit to Him, and He will make your paths straight."
- Proverbs 3:5–6

We never truly know what the next minute, hour, or day will bring. But God does. And in that truth, there is hope. The very moment ahead of us could hold the answer to a prayer we have been waiting on, the breakthrough we have been seeking, or the healing we need to stand back on our feet.

Life has a way of testing our patience, our strength, and sometimes even our faith. During those moments, it can feel easier to stop, to sit in discouragement, or to question whether anything will change. But Scripture reminds us that God is always working even when we cannot yet see the results.

"For we walk by faith, not by sight." — 2 Corinthians 5:7

Throughout life, many of us have heard someone say, "Even if you don't know what tomorrow will bring, don't sit around waiting in fear." Instead, hold onto faith and keep moving forward.

That wisdom still holds true today.

Progress does not always require knowing every detail about the future. Sometimes it simply requires trusting that God is guiding your steps one moment at a time.

So, if you are in a season of uncertainty, disappointment, or quiet struggle, remember this simple truth:

Everyone will not clap for your consistency.

Keep going anyway.

Most people won't keep their word.

Keep going anyway.

Everyone won't support you when you need them most.

Keep going anyway.

It may seem like you have lost everything.

Keep going anyway.

Many people will question your actions.

Keep going anyway.

You might be misunderstood in the beginning.

Keep going anyway.

You will hear No's more than often.

Keep going anyway.

You may not get any recognition or awards.

Keep going anyway.

People may talk bad about you when you're not around.

Keep going anyway.

You may not have any funding.

Keep going anyway.

People may walk away in the midst of the process.

Keep going anyway.

It may seem heavy in the moment.

Keep going anyway.

Nothing might not motivate you to get out the bed.

Keeping going anyway.

Because when you finally hit the mark for being resilient, brave, consistent, and fearless to see your vision come to life – you will be proud of YOU. And that's when you pause for a second and thank God.

Then proceed to continue to keep going!

God children shouldn't be scared or hesitant to bet on themselves and keep going. Increase your energy and vibration. Level up from the inside because that's where God dwells!

You become more of the person you always wanted to be or experience what you always yearned for when you just keep going.

SCRIPTURE TEACHES US

Galatians 6:9

"Let us not become weary in doing good, for at the proper time we will reap a harvest if we do not give up."

This scripture reminds us that persistence matters. Even when progress feels slow or invisible, God promises that faithfulness will eventually produce fruit.

Isaiah 40:31

"But those who hope in the Lord will renew their strength. They will soar on wings like eagles; they will run and not grow weary, they will walk and not faint."

This scripture reinforces the message of endurance. When we continue forward with hope in God, He provides renewed strength for the journey.

REFLECTIONS

What situation in my life right now requires me to trust God and keep moving forward even when I cannot see the full outcome?

How can I strengthen my faith daily so that discouragement does not cause me to stop before my breakthrough arrives?

PRAYER

Heavenly Father,
Thank You for reminding me that You see what I cannot see and know what lies ahead. When I feel tired, uncertain, or discouraged, renew my strength and help me continue forward in faith. Give me the courage to keep going even when the path is unclear. I trust that You are working in every moment of my life and that the answers I seek are already in Your hands. Amen.

GUARD YOUR BLESSINGS OR SUFFER IN YOUR HEAVEN

"Our kings, leaders, religious leaders, and fathers have not kept Your Law or listened to Your Laws and Your strong words which You have given them. Even when they were in their own nation, with all the good things You gave them and with the great rich land You gave them, they did not serve You or turn from their sins. See, we are servants today. We are servants in the land You gave to our fathers. You gave it to them so they could eat the fruit and have other good things. The many good things the land gives are used by the kings whom You have put over us because of our sins. They also rule over our bodies and over our cattle as they please. So we are in much trouble" - Nehemiah 9:34-37

God will bless us with riches, opportunities, and abundant provision in our "land of milk and honey." But when we fail to take responsibility for what He has entrusted to us, when we lack gratitude, or when we turn our hearts away from Him, even blessings can become a source of loss. HE will have us suffer in the same heaven He granted us on earth. What was once ours can be given into someone else's hands, leaving us to witness the fruits of our labor slipping away.

It is a deep pain to see your name on things you no longer steward, to hold scraps while others enjoy plenty, to watch abundance that was meant for you pass into the hands of others. It's a deep pain to have gold plates with scraps while witnessing others have plenty on paper plates.

Do not fall into the trap of abusing your privileges, assuming that God's provision is endless without accountability, or treating your blessings with disregard. To starve spiritually, emotionally, or materially in a land that God made abundant for you is a unique and profound disappointment.

Let gratitude, responsibility, and reverence guide how you manage what God has placed in your hands. Stewardship is more than possession; it is honoring the Source of your blessings.

SCRIPTURE TEACHES US

Proverbs 3:9-10

"Honor the Lord with your wealth, with the firstfruits of all your crops; then your barns will be filled to overflowing, and your vats will brim over with new wine."

True abundance comes when we give God honor and manage what He gives with reverence.

Luke 16:10-12

"Whoever can be trusted with very little can also be trusted with much, and whoever is dishonest with very little will also be dishonest with much... If you have not been trustworthy in handling worldly wealth, who will trust you with true riches?"

Faithful management of what God gives us in this life reflects our readiness for greater responsibility.

REFLECTIONS

In what areas of my life am I taking God's blessings for granted, and how can I practice better stewardship?

How can I cultivate gratitude and accountability so that what God has entrusted to me continues to grow rather than slip away?

PRAYERS

Heavenly Father,
Thank You for the blessings, opportunities, and abundance You have placed in my life. Help me to steward them with gratitude, humility,

and responsibility. Keep my heart aligned with You so I do not take Your provision for granted or let it slip away through neglect. Teach me to honor You in all I have, to manage wisely, and to serve faithfully. Protect my blessings and guide me to use them for Your glory. Amen.

MOVING QUIETLY (LESSONS FROM NEHEMIAH)

"Encourages private prayer and action rather than seeking public attention." - Matthew 6:6

Moving quietly and in silence is a skill that is often undervalued but it is essential for success. When people are not aligned with your vision, your goals, or your calling, sharing every detail of your plans can create unnecessary obstacles. God often calls us to act strategically and with discernment, protecting the work He has placed in our hands.

Spending time studying the book of *Nehemiah* gave me a deeper understanding of this principle, as well as insights about approval and spiritual alignment. Nehemiah was tasked with rebuilding the walls of Jerusalem, a monumental mission fraught with opposition. Though he received official approval from the ruling king, he never announced it to anyone, not one person knew of the king's permission. Instead, Nehemiah consistently emphasized that he had God's approval, and that alone was the strongest authorization one could receive.

This teaches us a powerful truth: nothing of lasting value moves without God's approval. Wealth, influence, resources, and even connections are only effective when God aligns them to support His purpose. Nehemiah's strength came from his daily connection with God through prayer, which created intimacy, clarity, and courage. He didn't waste time worrying or seeking validation from others; he prayed, discerned, and acted decisively.

Nehemiah's daily rhythm reminds us that we must Pray, Persevere, and Sacrifice to fulfill our calling. Opposition is inevitable. People may ridicule, mock, or try to discredit you to derail your progress. But just as Nehemiah faced public scorn and threats from Sanballat, Tobiah, and others - he remained focused, disciplined, and steadfast.

"When Sanballat heard that we were building the wall again, he became very angry. He was filled with anger and he made fun of the Jews... Tobiah the Ammonite was near him and said, 'If a fox would jump on what they build, he would break their stone wall down!'... Hear, O our God, how we are hated! Return their shame on their own heads. Let them be taken as servants to a strange land. Do not forgive their sin. Do not let their sin be covered from Your eyes. For they have made much fun of the builders." — **Nehemiah 4:1-5**

Whenever I am mocked, criticized, or ridiculed, I choose not to respond in kind or allow it to discourage me. Instead, I let it fuel me to continue the work God has entrusted to me. When your heart is pure and your intentions are aligned with God's will, opposition becomes a tool that sharpens your focus rather than a barrier to your success.

Like Nehemiah, we must:

- **Move quietly** - not broadcasting every plan, but trusting God to orchestrate the timing and outcome.
- **Stay anchored in prayer** - allowing God to guide decisions and provide wisdom.
- **Persist despite opposition** - turning criticism into motivation, and setbacks into lessons.

When you operate with this discipline, you position yourself for breakthroughs that others can only dream of. God honors diligence, humility, and faithfulness and He protects the work of your hands when you act in alignment with Him.

SCRIPTURE TEACHES US

Proverbs 16:3

"Commit to the Lord whatever you do, and he will establish your plans."

When we move quietly and align our actions with God, He ensures our work prospers according to His will.

Psalm 37:7

"Be still before the Lord and wait patiently for him; do not fret when people succeed in their ways, when they carry out their wicked schemes."

This reminds us that staying silent, patient, and faithful protects our focus and keeps us aligned with God's timing.

REFLECTIONS

What is one area in my life where I am sharing too much too soon, and how can I practice moving quietly with faith instead?

How can I use prayer, perseverance, and strategic action to stay focused on God's approval rather than seeking validation from others?

PRAYER

Heavenly Father,

Thank You for the lessons in Nehemiah's life. Teach me to move with wisdom and discernment, keeping my plans aligned with Your will. Help me to stay silent when necessary, persevere through opposition, and trust fully in Your approval. Guard my heart against discouragement, ridicule, and distractions, and give me the courage to act faithfully in every task You place before me. May all I do honor You and bring glory to Your name. In Jesus' name, Amen.

MY HARVEST
IS NOT ACCIDENTAL

"Then Jesus said to them, "Don't you understand this parable? How then will you understand any parable? The farmer sows the word. Some people are like seed along the path, where the word is sown. As soon as they hear it, Satan comes and takes away the word that was sown in them. Others, like seed sown on rocky places, hear the word and at once receive it with joy. But since they have no root, they last only a short time. When trouble or persecution comes because of the word, they quickly fall away. Still others, like seed sown among thorns, hear the word; but the worries of this life, the deceitfulness of wealth and the desires for other things come in and choke the word, making it unfruitful. Others, like seed sown on good soil, hear the word, accept it, and produce a crop some thirty, some sixty, some a hundred times what was sown."- Mark 4:13-20

God's harvest throughout our lives has always been abundant. Because of this, it is imperative that we are never weak witnesses of all He has done for us. We must boldly share the good news of how God blesses those who follow Him regardless of circumstances. Our testimony is seed. Our obedience is seed. Our consistency is seed.

To be a great farmer for God means we sow daily with authority, with faith, and without hesitation.

A farmer understands something critical: not every seed will land on good soil. Some will fall on hard ground. Some will land among rocks. Some will be choked by thorns. But great farmers do not stop sowing simply because some seeds will not grow. They sow generously because they know that enough will take root.

Likewise, we must increase how we sow into people, places, and opportunities - trusting God for the return.

- Sow many job applications → Position yourself for an offer.

- Make consistent fundraising asks → Reach your goal.
- Meet with more people → Expand your network.
- Stay consistent in service → Build loyalty and trust.
- The principle is simple: increased sowing increases opportunity for harvest.

But sowing is not just about effort, it is about endurance. We will encounter storms. We will face resistance. We will experience moments where it seems the seed is not producing.

Even the disciples underestimated Jesus while in the storm, despite witnessing His miracles (Mark 4:35–41). They panicked in the presence of power. Their proximity did not equal faith. This teaches us two things:

1. Even those close to you may not fully recognize the light and authority you carry.
2. Fear can blind people to what has already been proven.

When we understand the full capacity of someone or something, we treat it with faith and respect based on its track record. God has a flawless track record. Therefore, we sow with confidence.

There will be people who do not recognize your work, your calling, or your authority because they have not done their research. Let those moments become teaching moments. Our walk, our work, and our light are not of low value. We must operate in a way that reflects that.

We sow boldly because we trust God to multiply. We remain steady because we know He controls the harvest. And we move forward with faith, believing that the same God who calms storms will make space for our gifts to flourish.

Be a disciplined farmer. Sow daily. Protect the soil of your own heart. And trust that what is planted in faith will return in abundance.

SCRIPTURE REMINDS US

Galatians 6:7–9 (NIV)

"Do not be deceived: God cannot be mocked. A man reaps what he sows. Whoever sows to please the Spirit, from the Spirit will reap eternal life. Let us not become weary in doing good, for at the proper time we will reap a harvest if we do not give up."

This affirms both responsibility and endurance. The harvest is promised but persistence is required.

Ecclesiastes 11:6 (NIV)

"Sow your seed in the morning, and at evening let your hands not be idle, for you do not know which will succeed, whether this or that, or whether both will do equally well."

This scripture mirrors the farmer's mindset: sow consistently and trust God with the outcome. You don't control which seed produces, you control whether
you plant.

REFLECTIONS

Am I sowing consistently in the areas where I expect God to produce a harvest, or am I waiting for results without planting enough seed?

Has discouragement caused me to slow down in my sowing, and what would it look like to recommit to daily, disciplined planting?

PRAYER

Father God,

I come before You with the desire to be one of Your faithful farmers in this season. Thank You for equipping me with the tools necessary to tend to my own garden while also giving me seeds to sow into the lives of others.

Today, I ask that You align my heart with Yours. Teach me to sow deeply and faithfully into the good soil You place around me. Guide my hands and direct my steps so that I know where to go and where to plant.

I am grateful that You have chosen me to help expand Your territory and cultivate fields where Your wonders can be revealed. Continue to use me, Lord, so that I am never without good seed to sow, fruitful harvest to gather, and fertile soil to steward.

May everything I plant bring You glory.

Amen.

PERSONAL DEVOTIONAL WRITING

www.ingramcontent.com/pod-product-compliance
Lightning Source LLC
LaVergne TN
LVHW090603110826
845146LV00001B/239